LALA KENT

Give Them Lala

GALLERY BOOKS

New York London Toronto Sydney New Delhi

G

Gallery Books
An Imprint of Simon & Schuster, Inc.
1230 Avenue of the Americas
New York, NY 10020

First Gallery Books trade paperback edition April 2022

Some names have been changed, whether or not so noted in the text.

For information about special discounts for bulk purchases,
please contact Simon & Schuster Special Sales at 1-866-506-1949
or business@simonandschuster.com.

The Simon & Schuster Speakers Bureau can bring authors to your live event. For more information or to book an event, contact the Simon & Schuster Speakers Bureau at 1-866-248-3049 or visit our website at www.simonspeakers.com.

Interior design by Davina Mock-Maniscalco

10   9   8   7   6   5   4   3   2   1

The Library of Congress has cataloged the hardcover edition as follows:
Names: Kent, Lala, author.
Title: Give them Lala / Lala Kent.
Identifiers: LCCN 2020043649 (print) | LCCN 2020043650 (ebook) |
   ISBN 9781982153847 (hardcover) | ISBN 9781982153854 (trade paperback) |
   ISBN 9781982153861 (ebook)
Subjects: LCSH: Kent, Lala. | Vanderpump rules (Television program) | Women television
   personalities—United States—Biography. | Women alcoholics—United States—
   Biography. | Reality television programs—United States.
Classification: LCC PN1992.4.K474 A3 2021 (print) | LCC PN1992.4.K474 (ebook) |
   DDC 791.4302/8/092 [B]—dc23
LC record available at https://lccn.loc.gov/2020043649
LC ebook record available at https://lccn.loc.gov/2020043650

ISBN 978-1-9821-5384-7
ISBN 978-1-9821-5385-4 (pbk)
ISBN 978-1-9821-5386-1 (ebook)

This book is dedicated to those
courageous enough to be themselves.

contents

introduction

WHEN I FIRST STARTED using the phrase "Give them Lala," I was describing who Lauren Burningham, a girl from Salt Lake City, Utah, turned into when she was in front of the cameras on *Vanderpump Rules*. Unlike Lauren, Lala was confident, badass, and always did exactly what she wanted, for better or for worse . . . often worse, at least during my early seasons on the show.

Life moved fast after I entered the world of reality TV, and sometimes it's been hard for me to make sense of the present moment, let alone the past. Eventually, I reached a point where I had no choice but to stop, sit down with pen and paper, and take a long, hard look at myself. Lala made for good TV, that's for sure, but she was taking Lauren down some questionable paths. I needed to understand why. . . .

As a recovering addict working a program that continues to save my life, I've learned the importance of sharing the most vulnerable parts of myself with the people I love—my beloved family, my life partner, my fellow warriors in AA, and you, the fans. With your help, "Give them Lala" has evolved into something I can be proud of. And today, it's a reminder for me to *never* play a role and to always be the realest version of me, because the alternative leads to disaster.

So, here, I give you Lala. The real Lala, all of her, the good, the bad, and the ridiculous. There are things in these pages that even those closest to me do not know. I know the haters will continue to hate whatever I say or do, but that's okay—I'm opening up the contents of my heart anyway. Some names have been changed to protect the innocent and the not-so-innocent, and sorry not sorry to anyone I may offend along the way.

Love,
Lala

chapter one

THE H-WORD

*H*AVE YOU EVER BEEN slut-shamed? Ever been told your sexuality is offensive by someone who has no right to comment on it? Has anyone ever made a judgment call based on the way you dress, or the things you say? Have you ever been told to act like a lady, even though if we acted like the ladies those people wanted us to be we'd still be churning butter at home, waiting for a man to walk through the door? If so, you know how much it sucks to be on the receiving end of those judgments, by-products of a sexist narrative that has been shoved down our throats since we were little.

I've been judged and slut-shamed in a very public way, and never more so than when I was twenty-three, going through a period I call my ho phase, which was working out perfectly until the cameras got involved. A chunk of my ho-ness overlapped with my first season of filming *Vanderpump Rules*, meaning millions of people witnessed me living my very best-worst life—drunk, messy, and down for whatever. Take it from me, a lady's most shameless moments are much easier when they happen in private.

In case you're wondering, a ho phase goes a little something like this. You're at a club. You're feeling good. You see someone who gives you *those* kind of feels. You make eye contact, you start vibing, and suddenly you feel all happy down there. That is your body, calling them. Before long, the nips want a little attention; you're kissing and touching, and boom, it's like David Attenborough, mating-season-in-the-wild-type lovin'. Ideally the person you're about to bump pee-pees with is a friend, or a friend of a friend, because I don't condone slipping off with a stranger and having sex with them. Be smart, be safe, and feel free to never deny yourself a good lay—I didn't. When I was ho-phasing, if I was attracted to him and we were vibing, it was going down.

There is no such thing as being "too old" to go through this phase, by the way. There are women I know who married young and are experiencing a ho phase for the first time, in their forties, which I love. I know some women who have had more than one ho phase, which is wonderful, too. There's no right or wrong time to do it, although one advantage of being sexually free in your twenties is that it allows you to really figure out what you like and what you don't like, relatively early on in the game. Then, when you meet someone you're compatible with, you'll know.

To this day, I look back on my ho phase as a period of major growth. It gave me confidence; it helped me release a relationship I had been desperately hanging on to; it gave me a power that every woman should experience. Most of all, my ho phase was the bridge to the happy home I share with my soul mate, Randall, whose last name I cannot wait to share. In many ways, ho-ing really is the path to enlightenment.

Even so, ho-phasing can be challenging. Hearts get broken, feelings get burned, and lines get blurred. You might start second-guessing yourself, or worrying what other people think. You do run the high risk of being judged and slut-shamed when you're a woman who's sexually free because, unfortunately, that's just how our society works, and it sucks. People judge women more harshly than they judge men, and at times, you may even find you're judging yourself.

If you start feeling this way, disengage. Take a time-out and reflect. If ho-phasing no longer feels right, maybe it's because you've reached the end of your phase, or maybe ho-phasing wasn't really meant for you at all. I know many girls in Salt Lake who are naturally wholesome, who never needed to explore their sexuality with multiple partners. But if you're like me, then maybe you like experimenting . . . maybe you've gotten drunk, and maybe you've eaten a cookie or two . . . Just know I love you, and there is no judgment here, ever. Do you, boo. Just maybe don't do it on TV, like I did.

Had I been given the choice, I never would have chosen to go through this time on camera. Some days it felt like the whole world was calling me names they would probably never have called a man in my same position. My ho phase was life changing, but it also came at a huge cost to my mental health. Girls projected their closeted ho hatred onto me, as did the very dudes who were trying to sleep with me (but never could). Not to mention the online trolls. From trolls, fans, and cast alike, the one word that came up over and over again was *whore*.

I was called a "ratchet whore," a "gold-digging whore," . . . and the one that hurt me the most: "home-wrecking whore." I always say, if you're going to call me a name, at least be accurate. Call me a raging bitch whose mouthy ass may or may not need "several good throat punches and an ass kicking," as someone suggested on a Reddit thread once. Call me a drunk, because, yes, hi, I'm Lala, and I'm an alcoholic. Call me angry; call me someone who needs to pull her shit together—I am all of those things—but don't call me a whore, because a whore is someone who gets paid to have sex, which would be dope, but I don't and never have.

For a twenty-three-year-old girl from Utah named Lauren Burningham, who suddenly found herself backed into a corner by strangers calling her every name under the sun, it was an intimidating and scary time to be alive. This was not my first rodeo when it came to big, bad bitches—I had dealt with bullies since elementary school—but the hate I got on my first season of *Vanderpump* was anxiety-triggering on a whole other level. The choice was simple—quit the show and save my sanity, or buck the hell up and find new ways to cope.

Every day I walked into SUR, my self-defense mechanisms were on ten, my sharp tongue was ready to destroy, and my short fuse was set to blow. Later, I'd find my secret weapon—a liquid that allowed me to numb myself, give no fucks, and clap back to any insult with the most shady, most outrageous, most below-the-belt dig ever. Alcohol helped me KO my slut-shaming enemies each and every time, resulting in unforgettable TV (if I do say so myself), but watching it back, I'd hate myself and feel embarrassed for what I'd said and done, even though at the time, fighting back was just a matter of survival.

Reality TV plus slut-shaming plus alcohol turned young, sensitive, insecure Lauren Burningham into a badder, madder version of herself—Lala Kent, super-bitch bully-crusher who always came out guns a-blazing . . . and sometimes shot herself in the foot. If Lala hadn't existed, Lauren might have lasted a few seasons on *Vanderpump* before giving up her Hollywood dreams and going back to Utah, traumatized, to settle down with a local boy. But that wasn't in the cards. . . .

I vividly remember the day I told my parents I was moving to LA. I drove down to the Humane Society of Utah in Salt Lake

City, where my mom, Lisa, works. My dad, Kent, was there helping her put together their annual fundraiser. I screeched into the parking lot like I was in *The Fast and the Furious* and marched in to give them the big news.

"Just so you know, I'm moving to LA next week," I said, acting casual, even though in my mind I was screaming, "I'M MOVING TO LA AND GETTING OUT OF THIS CLOSED-MINDED PLACE, AND YOU GUYS WILL NOT STOP ME!"

"That's great, Lauren!" said my mom.

I don't think she believed me—I had already tried living in LA before, when I was nineteen, and had lasted only six months, for reasons I'll explain. But this time, I was twenty-three and I felt different. Stronger. I was going to grow some balls (ovaries, rather) and go to Hollywood, where I would make it as an actor, my dream since I was a little girl. This time, I wasn't going to be intimidated by the process, or take rejection personally. Most important, I was going to kick my anxiety's ass. Insecurities be gone!

The following week, with one suitcase and $2,000 in my bank account, I hopped in my friend Janet's car (she was also in search of the big dream-come-true), and we hauled ass to Hollywood. We split a $200 one-bedroom sublet in Alhambra, a pretty quiet part of the city, about an hour away from everything. After a couple of months, Janet went back to Utah and it was time to find a real place to live. My friend Danielle, older sister of my best friend and soul sister, Madison, who I grew up with in Utah and also lives in

LA, told me someone she knew was looking for a roommate. The apartment was in Miracle Mile, and my portion of the rent would be $900 a month, which I could afford because I was a big-time saver—I had been working since I was twelve, and had shoved all my money away in a savings account, ready for a moment like this. I moved in the next day.

The two-bedroom, two-bathroom apartment was on the corner of Olympic and Hauser. It got very little light, and the decor was beyond depressing. My bathroom had burgundy tile with peach trim, and the shower was too small to bend over in to shave your legs.

My roommate, Megan, was a bag of fun and didn't care about the apartment being in disarray. She kept her cat's litter box in the laundry room, which made me spiral, daily. I would move the shit box into her bathroom every morning when she went to school, even though as soon as she got home, it would end up back in the laundry room. Bills often went unopened, and rarely was her half of the rent paid on time. I'm a Virgo, and I could deal with cleaning up the apartment, but the rent issue was too much—my name was on the lease, and I was terrified of my credit tanking.

"Your credit is your name," my mom always told me, just like her father had always told her.

I had to make sure I could afford the whole rent and bills at the top of the month, just in case Megan couldn't—anything to keep my credit looking snatched—so I set my mind on finding a job as soon as possible. I got a fit modeling job for $40 an hour, meaning I was a living mannequin, being photographed in various outfits that would go on clothing companies' e-commerce sites. I would wake up at 6:00 a.m. Monday through Friday to get fully glammed and get to downtown LA by eight. Models usually worked no more than two days a week for just four hours at a time, because believe it or not, fit modeling is exhausting work. But I hustled the agency into letting me work every day, for as many hours as the state of California would allow. I would change outfits between seventy-five to one hundred times a day and have my picture taken. I'd always show up in perfect makeup, camera ready, although most of the time, my head would get chopped off in editing. But all in all, despite the long hours and exhaustion, I wasn't mad that this was my moneymaking situation, because being a fit model meant I didn't have to work at a restaurant like everyone else in town. Since I was a little kid, being a server seemed like the hardest job in the entire world, and was the *last* thing I wanted to do. Ironic, I know.

Some days, after a particularly long day of modeling, I'd wonder why I'd left my mom and dad's chic home in Salt Lake City, then I'd remind myself, this was one step along the road to the acting dreams I'd had since I was a little girl. I wished I could have been more laser-focused on making those dreams come true, but there was something distracting me from pursuing auditions . . . my on-again, off-again relationship with this snack-and-a-half linebacker named Carter Hoffman. He played college football in LA, was on his way to entering the 2015 NFL draft, and was the second real boyfriend I'd ever had. Physically, Carter was the sexiest thing I had ever seen in my entire life. And he had me wrapped around his finger.

It's funny—when I was younger, if you'd asked me or my friends what we looked for in a partner, nine times out of ten we wouldn't talk about how that person treated us or how they made us feel. It would be all about their facial features, what they did for a living, or how much money they had. It's rare that you hear a young woman say, "I want someone who takes care of my heart and cares about my feelings," because those things just aren't a priority. Carter checked all the boxes of what I wanted at the time, and hardly any of what I needed, and I couldn't shake him for the life of me. Each time he broke my heart, I went back for more, until one day, he pushed me too far, triggering the start of my ho phase, for all the world to see.

Carter and I had gotten together when I was twenty-one and he was nineteen. I was still living in Utah, and he would fly me out to LA often, which in the beginning felt super sweet and romantic. But the balance of power shifted quickly, which often happens when a dude gets too comfortable. Carter had a big ego and started treating me like I was some clueless little Utah girl. Which in a way, I was. I had a ton of insecurities and let a lot of his bad behavior slide because I was always trying to be the cool bitch who didn't stress out about things too much. Big mistake. Only be a cool bitch if you really are a cool bitch, that's my advice. Otherwise you're just setting yourself up for disaster by hiding what you really feel.

Each time I visited, it seemed like Carter behaved with less and less respect toward me. I would fly out to watch his games, and afterward, instead of celebrating with me, he'd ask if he could go out with "just the boys." In my head I'd be thinking, *Are you kidding me?* But the words never came out like that.

I'd say, "Yes, of course, baby, you deserve it. Y'all played great!"

Then the pit in my stomach would sink in, and I'd just hope that because I was being such a "cool girlfriend," it would make him want to treasure me forever. How naive I was.

It was on one of those visits that I felt the power of intuition for the first time. That feeling you get when something just isn't right. It's like nothing else, and I've come to learn, it's all we can really trust. Carter and I were at the house he shared with five other dudes, who were also on the football team. He told me he needed to study for tests that were coming up, and, of course, I was totally okay with this. I told him I would call my Utah homie in LA and kick it with her until he was finished. He headed to campus around 1:00 p.m., and said he'd be back in a few hours.

Nighttime fell, and I sent a few casual texts asking when he'd be done; those texts went unanswered. I blew up his phone once midnight rolled around, and when he finally answered the phone at 12:30 a.m. he promised he was on his way to pick me up from my friend's place, which was about twenty minutes from his school campus at that hour of night. I tried to maintain my cool-bitch facade. But once 1:30 a.m. hit, I was way less chill.

"Where the fuck are you, Carter?" I said.

"I just got pulled over by the cops, Lauren."

I hung up, feeling uneasy. Something felt off. Then 2:00 a.m. approached and I'd heard no word, so I gave him another call.

"This is ridiculous. You've been MIA all day. What the fuck is going on?"

"Calm down, La. It's been a long day, and now I have a flat tire I gotta change!"

After hanging up, I looked at my friend and gave her my exact prediction on what would happen when he showed up. "I'm going to ask to see the ticket he got when he was pulled over, and he is going to say the cop let him off the ticket because he plays football. But there will be a tire in the back seat, because that is karma for his bullshit. And he is going to make me feel stupid for being suspicious when he has been 'working his ass off all day.'"

I knew Carter very well by now, and every single one of the things I predicted transpired, in that order, when he finally arrived to pick me up at three thirty in the morning, including the part where he guilt-tripped me and made me feel like an asshole for questioning him. But I was too tired to push the matter. I just wanted to sleep.

Once we got home, I went straight up the stairs to his bedroom, immediately noticing that his bed was unmade, which was weird because I had definitely made it before we both left the house. I saw that my suitcase had been shoved into his closet, as if to cover up that I was staying there, and my blanket that I traveled with everywhere was shoved in between the couch cushions.

"Why is my stuff shoved away like this, Carter? Why is the bed unmade? Who was here?!"

"My boy brought a girl over and used my room."

"I don't believe you! I think *you* brought someone back here and wanted to cover that shit up!"

We battled back and forth before I completely exhausted myself and he shut down. This was how it always went with us, and by the time we got in bed, the sun was beginning to rise. Carter fell asleep fast, but I couldn't. My gut was churning, and I felt like a hundred knives were being shoved and turned in my back. There's a real, physical pain you get deep in your gut when you know someone is lying, and it was a pain I never wanted to feel again. In fact, this very moment set the tone for my future relationships, because never again would I allow myself to ignore that feeling. Never.

When Carter woke up, he said he was getting his hair cut and then he would take me to lunch to "make up for last night."

Nope, I thought. I was taking my ass to LAX, catching the next flight back to Salt Lake, and I wasn't even going to tell him my plan. He was going to get back from his haircut and wonder, *Where the hell is Lauren?* Which is exactly how it went down.

When I moved to LA in 2013, we were still dating on and off. I couldn't quit him. Carter was someone I loved and wanted, and now that I was actually living in the same city as him, I figured things could be different. He had matured, I had toughened up, and our biggest problem—the distance between us—had now been solved! I was an LA resident; let's get it poppin', daddy.

I played hard to get for a few weeks. Then he invited me over to his new place, which was no longer occupied by five other football players. This was a relief—there's nothing less sexy than having sex when you know five other people in the house know you're having sex.

I had butterflies all day before seeing him, and when he met me at the door and kissed me, I knew. *This is it. This is how I want to feel for the rest of my life.* We walked hand in hand up the stairs to his bedroom. I stepped in and looked over to the bed. Again, that sinking feeling hit me as I saw a pair of hoops on the nightstand, and next to them, a used condom. Yes, you read that correctly. Used. Condom.

My feelings of happy anticipation vanished. I felt nauseated, and fought back the tears as I said, voice trembling, "Really, dude? You don't even respect me enough to clean up your mess from the last bitch?"

I turned around, rushed back down the stairs, and out the

door to my car. I waited there, crying, hoping he would chase me, or call me, or something. But he didn't. He let me stand there, waiting for him, like he always had. He was telling me, *This is who I am, and you need to accept that.* But I couldn't accept this level of disrespect from someone I had so much history with. I just couldn't.

I drove home—by this time, Megan had moved out and Danielle had moved in, which I was thrilled about, because we had known each other our entire lives. (As my best friend's older sister, she was the closest thing to family I had out in LA.) I told her what had happened with Carter, the gross used condom, and she gave me the "fuck him, he doesn't deserve you" talk that all girlfriends give one another when guys do something messed up. She was right, I did deserve better. I was sick of being taken for granted. Sick of crying and wishing for more. I was done being humiliated. It was time for a new chapter.

That afternoon, Danielle and I rolled up to Costco to stock up on some essentials—vodka, food, and more vodka—and as I passed the personal care aisle, something caught my eye, a thing that all educated hos require in their toolbox. Trojan Magnum condoms. I got the largest box they had. Back at Olympic and Hauser, I cleaned out the top drawer of my nightstand and dumped all the condoms inside. Now, it was time to execute.

Danielle and I decided to go to Hyde, a club on Sunset Boulevard in West Hollywood. I knew it was going to be a good night because "California Love" by Tupac and Dre was playing when we walked in—something about that song always makes me feel myself. We sat at a table with hot dudes, the ones who always snagged the new blood that came to LA. These guys were promoters, friends of promoters, actors, friends of actors, heirs, friends of heirs. They never changed, but the lineup of girls who sat at their table did. Later on in my ho phase I would let a few of them hit it. But that night, my eye was on the security guy. . . . He was about six foot five, built like Dwight Howard, and was giving me tingles in *all* the right places.

Danielle said his name was Marquis and vouched for him, saying he was a good dude—this was important information for me. Like I said before, when you're in a ho phase, try to be safe and stick with the guys who are known among your group of friends. Do your homework before you give them "the look." Which I did, several times.

I got up to use the restroom, and as I slipped by him he grabbed my hand and leaned in closely. "Let me walk with you to keep you safe."

Can you bend me over while you're at it? I thought.

He walked me to and from the ladies' room, holding my hand. It was poppin' from there. I continued to give him baby-making eyes, and he continued to smile at me and ask me if I was doing okay. Before I dipped, I asked him for his number. I had never been this assertive with a guy before. He gave me his digits and asked me to call his phone so he could save mine. The moment I left, I texted him:

Come over when you're off work.

He did, and as soon as he walked in the door, we went to bang town. This was my first (and only) one-night stand. The first notch on my ho belt.

I loved it, but despite my successful ho moment with Marquis, my heart wasn't fully committed to the phase. I was sad, the crying-in-bed-with-my-blankie-watching-back-to-back-*Friends* kind of sad. It took a visit from my mom and some words of her wisdom to whip me back into shape and get me back in the ho saddle.

"Listen," she said. "I came out to California to have a nice time, but you're ruining it for me over some guy! You need to get over him!"

The penny dropped. I had to cut Carter off and move on and finally break the emotional and physical bond I'd built with him over the last three years. Hooking up with as many people as possible seemed like a reasonable way to do it. It helped, of course, that I had a ho door.

The ho door opened directly into my bedroom from the outside. Therefore, visitors didn't have to walk through the apartment to get into my room. This really came in handy when, every once in a while, I'd bag one dude, then have him make a quick exit so the newer, hotter dude could come through. Not every ho's bedroom has a literal revolving door, but if you can figure one into your architecture, I'd highly recommend it.

Because I was always a safe and educated ho, every hookup felt like a positive experience—for me, anyway. But there were a few times I hurt a guy's feelings—when you're ho-phasing, it's easy to do that, because you're not invested and it's all just a game. Also, because I had been rejected for three years, I'd forgotten that men had feelings, too, that their hearts needed to be handled with care sometimes. I wasn't always great at that.

Which brings me to André Smith, a banger from Baltimore. Built like Ray Lewis and covered in tattoos, he had dreadlocks down his back and was a perfect snack. I knew him from back home, where he played football at the University of Utah. We had had sexy time on a few occasions, and it had really helped me get my mind off Carter during one of the worst times in our relationship a few years back. So when André told me he was moving to LA and asked if he could crash at my place for a while until he got situated, I said yes, temporarily forgetting that I was supposed to be living in a rhythm with no attachments. My bad.

Before André arrived, I cleaned out one side of my closet, which was basically the size of a coat closet, and three drawers. André arrived, unpacked, lined his sneakers up against my wall, and just like that I went from a ho phase to HOLY SHIT I HAVE A LIVE-IN BOYFRIEND. After he was situated, it was time to lay out the ground rules—I told André I had no interest in being exclusive, but I also didn't want to disrespect him by sleeping with him and someone else in the same night. At the time, this seemed like a rock-solid plan, and André said he was cool with it.

That first night, André said he was going to say what's up to his sister in downtown LA and would probably stay the night there. I loved this idea, since I had already made plans with a yummy man named Cooper. After a lot of drinks, I brought Cooper home and let him hit it. He was super cool, so I didn't mind him sleeping over afterward.

At 5:00 a.m., I got a phone call from André. I told Cooper to shh and then answered.

"Hey, babe."

"Hey, boo. I'm pulling up. Can you unlock the door?"

"What? How far away are you?"

"I'm here. Just parked."

Shit! I hung up, made sure the ho door was locked, and told Cooper to go in Danielle's room. (Cooper and Danielle were old friends, so I knew she wouldn't be too freaked out by him crawling into her bed.) André knocked on the ho door, and I let him in. He climbed into my bed and got lovey with me, but I just couldn't do it. My conscience was stepping in, making me feel like a shitty person. André was a piece of home, I respected him. I had to tell him the truth.

"André, I can't do this tonight."

"Why, baby, what's up?"

"Because I brought a dude home and he's hiding in Danielle's room."

I pulled the covers over my head, wishing I would have shut the fuck up and not said anything. I felt André leap out of bed and barge into Danielle's room, ready to go toes with Cooper.

Danielle sprung to Cooper's defense, pushing André (unsuccessfully) and yelling, "Get the fuck out of my room! Leave!" Danielle may be a tiny human, but when she gets mad, it is absolutely terrifying.

André stormed back into my bedroom and started packing up, much quicker than he had unpacked. As he opened the ho door, arms full of his belongings, he left me with these immortal words:

"You could have been with a millionaire."

I tried reaching out a few times after to apologize but never got a response. Sadly, we never spoke again. This is what we refer to as a ho fail. But I had started to notice something—the less invested I was in building a relationship, the more my "lovers" seemed to want me. How in the hell is that supposed to make sense? Why was it that if I showed a guy I was ride-or-die for him, he was less attracted, but if I treated him like a piece of meat, that's when he was blowing up my phone, beating my door down for a moment of my time? I began to understand why people say you should "act like a woman and think like a man," because apparently it drives some guys wild when you don't give a shit about them.

I started to understand some of the mistakes I had been making with Carter, like continuing to sleep with him despite the way he treated me. To this day, I tell my friends, if you feel an emotional connection toward someone who isn't offering you what you need in return, you *must* stop having sex with them. Trust me, boo, it always ends in tears. It can be so hard to do; I know that. Sometimes a dude gives you just enough to allow him the pussy, and you feel wanted for twenty minutes, maybe longer if you're lucky, and then you're left feeling emptier than you felt before the bang sesh. Reject him, ladies! Send him away. They need to go above and beyond for your cookie.

By the mid stage of my ho phase, I was incapable of emotionally attaching to anyone and was breaking hearts without ever meaning to. But I didn't care. I had really come into my own and was having a great time. The moments I thought about Carter were few and far between. Sex was just fun, and if anyone tried to get too clingy with me, they were in for a rude awakening.

I kept hearing through our group of friends that this hot actor guy named Cody was cyberstalking me and hoping for an introduction. *Why not?* I thought. A mutual friend linked us up through text, and Cody and I decided to set a date for Valentine's Day. Meeting someone for the first time on V Day is unusual and a little aggressive, I know, but I figured with enough edibles and vino, we'd forget what day it was and just have an epic time before I sent him back out through the ho door. Which is exactly what happened. We drank, got stoned out of our minds, and had sex all over the apartment. It was one of the most fun Valentine's Days I've ever had.

At some point during the night he went to the bathroom. When he came back to bed, he made a comment about the lack of toilet paper in my bathroom. For a girl in her early twenties, experiencing her first ho phase, grocery-store runs are low on the to-do list.

"I guess I'm more of a baby wipes kind of chick?" I said, and didn't think anything more of it.

I liked Cody. He seemed easygoing. But a couple of nights later, I learned that unless he'd eaten several pot cookies, Cody was *not* chill. I invited him to my friend's house in the Hollywood Hills and he was mad at me for being stoned. (During my ho phase, I was always stoned on edibles.) He followed me around the party, disapproving of my life choices, and it was starting to make me feel claustrophobic. I wished he would let loose and mingle, but he wasn't having it. He kept saying he wanted alone time with me, even though I was in absolutely no state to have a serious conversation—I was baked, high on living my best life. He bugged me so much, I sent him home and told him I would call him later. He was super bent by this, and then, I completely spaced on calling him because I was too high to remember he existed.

The next day, Cody called me and said we weren't compatible. Duh. I agreed. At the end of our breakup conversation, he said, "Can I come by later to drop off some edibles? You might as well have them, since I don't do them as much."

Danielle and I were broke, and if someone was offering me free edibles, I was taking them.

Later that day, Cody pulled up outside my place, handed me a bag, and drove off without saying a word. *Weird.* Then I looked at the bag—printed on it, in big letters, were the words *FUCK YOU.* Inside, a lot of edibles . . . and a roll of toilet paper. Low blow! I was shook. Clearly, Cody was very upset; "fuck you" gift bags don't grow on trees, and he must have worked hard to find it.

Danielle and I couldn't stop laughing—it was a ridiculous, unnecessary thing for Cody to do and deserved a ridiculous, unnecessary reaction. I waited about forty-five minutes before calling him—I wanted to make sure he'd gotten all the way home first.

"Baby, I really want to make this right," I said. "Can you please come back so we can talk?"

Forty-five minutes later, he pulled up outside my apartment. I walked out, the "FUCK YOU" bag in my hand. Inside was the toilet paper. No edibles. Danielle and I needed those—the struggle is real out here in California. I opened his car door and threw it in.

"You're thirty-five years old, Cody. Act like it."

By this point, Carter was starting to send me messages, all of which remained unanswered. He had done a real number on my heart, but I was finally over it and ready to give him a taste of his own medicine. I finally responded and told him to come over. Carter was about to step into some unfamiliar waters. I was Lala now. And Lala was a beast.

Carter showed up, and without further ado, the condom drawer was opened. Afterward, I took the used condom and held it up. "This is what you do with a condom when you're finished with it, Carter, in order to show respect to the next person who comes over." I walked into the bathroom, dropped it in the toilet, and flushed. "Carter, this is what I'll do with every condom I use, so you never have to see something that might make you feel uncomfortable. That's called respect."

My words shook him. His face said it all: *Oh shit. She's flushing used condoms from other dudes?*

I was much more assertive than the girl from Utah he'd once known, and, predictably, he was very attracted to that. I got back in bed, expecting him to leave, but this time he wanted to cuddle and watch a movie, instead of leaving right after, as he always had. Now it was my turn to be shook.

Who is this person? And why are guys so weird?

Carter slept over that night. And from then on, he was attentive. He now invited me out with his friends and wanted me by his side at dinner. If I said no to meeting him at the club, he'd offer to take a separate Uber from his friends to pick me up first. He began giving me the affection and attention I'd always wanted, but it was too late. I had changed, and my inner ho was steering the ship. She stuck up for me. She was bossy and badass. She encouraged me to celebrate my sexuality. She helped me heal my heart, and thanks to her, my mental health was good. For the first time since meeting Carter, I felt happy and whole. No way was I going to risk that, no matter how sweetly he was behaving.

When he invited me out, I'd say I had to be up early. When he asked me to dinner, I'd say I already made plans. I did whatever I could to keep him in my "ho box." I couldn't allow myself to get attached. I'd come too far to fall back. Meanwhile, Carter fell madly in love with me. Actually, he fell in love with Lala, the bad bitch who was ho-phasing and about to get famous on TV, not Lauren, the sensitive little girl from Utah who would have done anything for him. That's why I could never take him seriously— because if you can't love me at my Lauren, you sure as hell don't deserve me at my Lala.

chapter two

REALITY TV SAVED MY SOUL

$\mathcal{S}$UR—THE "SEXY UNIQUE RESTAURANT" in West Hollywood where *Vanderpump Rules* is shot—is the mother ship, the heart of everything. No matter where me and the other cast members end up in life, SUR will always be the place where it all started.

I first went to SUR at the age of eighteen, long before I ever joined the cast of the show, before it was taken over by Ken Todd and Lisa Vanderpump. Danielle and Madison, the sisters I'd grown up with in Utah, both worked there, and it was our go-to dinner-and-drinks spot whenever I came out to visit. It looked very different back then: quaint and chic, much smaller and less grand than it is now. I was familiar with all the servers there, including some of the *Vanderpump* OGs, like Jax. (Fun fact—I was present when Jax and Stassi met for the first time, in Las Vegas, two years before the show was even picked up by Bravo.)

When I arrived in LA at age twenty-three, Danielle hooked me up with an evening job at SUR. I was terrified of the service industry, but I needed the extra cash. It was easily the most stressful experience of my working life, and the whole thing came crashing to an end when, one night, I made a group of "somebodies" wait at the bar for their table. Big mistake. They were insulted and complained to Diana, the Bulgarian bombshell manager, who ripped me a brand-new asshole. I wasn't committed enough to my job to stand for that, so I grabbed my things from underneath the hostess stand, headed to the back, clocked out, and exited through the infamous back alley. No way was I going to be spoken to that way. I had lasted literally three shifts. Later on in my SUR career, Diana would become one of my favorite human beings. But that night, if you told me I'd one day work at SUR again, I would have laughed in your face. Never in a million years.

Fast-forward to 2015, the summer before my twenty-fifth birthday. I was ho-phasing my little heart out, trying to get over Carter and get ahead in Hollywood, while fit modeling every hour of the day, in between auditions. My manager sent me to a casting for a Target commercial, and I had high hopes; until I filled out the sign-in sheet at the audition, which wanted to know how many followers I had on Instagram and Twitter. *The hell?*

I didn't have a Twitter account. I had all of three hundred followers on Instagram. I looked at the other actors' numbers, which blew my "following" out of the water. Fear set in. *Is this what acting's about now? Your social media following?* I looked up some of the other girls' names on the 'gram, and sure enough, some of them had followings in the tens of thousands. I couldn't compete.

After the audition I headed home, where Danielle was getting ready for her shift at SUR. I had a minor meltdown about my future, so to cheer me up, Danielle told me to come to work with her that night at the restaurant.

"I'll get you free drinks," she said.

I was in.

At SUR, I drowned my sorrows, lifted my spirits, and flitted around the room like a butterfly. Give Lala a few drinks, and she's working the room, uninhibited, making new best friends whose names she won't remember the next morning. Lisa Vanderpump noticed me doing my thing, and made her way over to me in the lounge. Six-inch heels, flawless makeup, head-to-toe designer wear—picture Lisa in the opening titles of *Vanderpump*, that's who floated toward me, smiling, that night. Lisa told me they were looking for a hostess and with that hostess gig came the possibility of appearing on *Vanderpump Rules*. Was I interested? I was tipsy, and it took a second before her words sank in.

I knew Lisa as the star of *The Real Housewives of Beverly Hills*, and obviously I'd heard about the show's spin-off *Vanderpump Rules*, which followed the waitstaff at SUR and was building a devoted fan following thanks to its specific kind of realness. But I wasn't much of a reality TV fan. And I'd never even seen one episode of *Vanderpump*, although I did remember hearing about it when it was about to launch on Bravo and saying to my mom, "Who the hell is going to watch that? I can't think of anything less interesting than watching a bunch of servers."

How wrong I was.

People have tried to re-create *Vanderpump Rules* a million times over, and the imitators usually don't even make it to a second season. There's something unique about the history and bond each *Vanderpump* cast member has with one another. Everyone had dated, slept together, made out, or lived together a decade before the show existed. They have all done the most fucked-up things to one another, and are still ride-or-die, nonetheless. Those are not relationships you can easily just manufacture.

But when Lisa offered me the job, I hesitated. I was a theater geek and my goal was to be a part of the scripted world of film and television. Sure, I used to watch *Laguna Beach* and *Bad Girls Club*, but never had I aspired to the unscripted life. Cameras following me around, broadcasting my most intimate moments? Hell no. That sounded horrifying to me. Plus, the pay on a reality TV show is pennies compared to when you book a scripted role. Just saying.

So, when Lisa made me the offer, my first thought was *RUN, LAUREN, RUN*. Then I thought about it—after being in LA for nearly two years, all I'd booked was a Buick commercial and a handful of indie films. I thought about that Target sign-in sheet. *Followers* . . . I needed followers. Maybe a season of reality TV would boost my profile, get my name out there, just enough that I'd become a "someone." Carter had been picked up in the NFL draft, and I was obsessing over it, because he was making moves like he'd always planned, whereas I was still going nowhere fast.

Fuck it, I thought. *I'm doing it. My talent will be seen if it is meant to be seen.* With nothing to lose, I swallowed my pride and decided to give reality a chance.

My first day of filming, I was shitting bricks. *Do I look okay? Will they like me?*

Lisa came up to me while the cameras were rolling and asked how my first day was going.

My answer was "No one's punched me in the face or called me a bitch yet—"

And Lisa responded, "Well, that's good."

Most of my friends think I'm really funny, so I figured my cast-mates would, too. Not so much. The first scene I ever filmed, I walked to a long wooden table where established cast members Katie Maloney and Scheana Shay were sitting.

"Hi, I'm Lala," I said.

They were acting very aloof, giving off top-of-the-food-chain energy, and it only went downhill from there. It would be nearly two years before I got anything close to a genuine smile out of those girls. Katie Maloney, especially . . . I mean, these days, just the thought of her makes my heart explode with love, but we had the rockiest start. We both have a tongue that will slice you like a Samurai sword. And we both came from Utah, which just goes to show: non-Mormon bitches from Utah don't play.

Right before joining *Vanderpump*, a rich, super-famous actor who shall remain unnamed had invited me alongside a bunch of other hot chicks to vacation on his yacht in Italy. Sipping rosé on a yacht in Lake Como sounded like a dream, except now I had this damn SUR job. I made up a little white lie so I could get out of my shifts for a week and told Lisa I had to go to Italy for a high-fashion modeling job. Listen, I'm five foot six and no Adriana Lima, but all I cared about was having a solid enough excuse to gain Lisa's permission to get the time off work. I had no idea this little lie, combined with my Instagram profile picture (a nude shot of my back side with my hands squeezing my ass) would result in so much anger and drama between me and the other girls on the show.

"So what do you have to do for that free trip?" Scheana asked me, all innocent.

"Luckily, I'm just a fun bitch to be around, so I get to keep my legs closed," I said, trying to be funny.

"But what about your mouth?"

Scheana really tried to give me a tough time, which must have been a lot of work for her, because she can be very sweet, and when she tries to bully people, it's uncomfortable to watch. But, of course, I didn't know that about her at the time. All I knew was that she was acting like she hated me, almost as much as Katie seemed to. They were so rude to me about my fake modeling trip, I canceled the whole thing and spent my time off in Utah, crying on my mom's shoulder, gathering up the strength to go back and face these people at work.

Katie's boyfriend, Tom Schwartz, a model and bartender at SUR, kept his distance, although with time, I'd learn that Schwartzy is like the cast's little puppy—when he bites it hurts, but he is too damn cute to get mad at. The other Tom, Tom Sandoval, made up the other half of the Tom-Tom bromance. There were times I really wanted to knock him off his high horse, shake him and say, "Listen, you make mistakes, too!" But then we would have a deep conversation about something like the art of shaving, and I'd fall hard—Tom Sandoval is a straight dude who loves hair products, a good suit, and who taught me the ultimate way to exfoliate your face is to shave it. To this day, I shave my face weekly, thanks to him.

In my first season, Sandoval was usually too busy arguing with his girlfriend, bartender Ariana Madix, to even notice me. Ariana is a badass blonde bombshell with an ass that won't quit, and for a while, she was the one girl who kept me afloat because she defends the underdog at all costs. Which, when you're the underdog, feels great.

There was one other new girl, Faith Stowers, so we agreed to have each other's backs, because everyone else at SUR seemed like they were so psycho—intensely loyal to one another yet full of beef from prior seasons. Too much drama for me, so I figured "you do you, I'll do me" over here, behind the hostess station. I smiled politely, seated diners, and tried not to get in trouble with Diana, the Bulgarian manager who remembered me from the last time I'd worked there.

The only people who were nice to me those first few days were the skinny British DJ, James Kennedy, who had coined himself the "White Kanye," and Jax Taylor, the Derek Zoolander of SUR with the bangin' bod and insatiable curiosity for what was underneath the clothes of every girl who walked into the restaurant. Both James and Jax were nothing but adorable to me because, yes, they had ulterior motives—but my policy is, I don't care *why* you're nice to me, I just care that you're nice to me. I had no idea that both of them had girlfriends, and when they flirted with me, I flirted right back. I'd never experienced this level of duplicity among men. It's just not how we roll in Utah. Back home, if someone has a girlfriend, they're usually honest about it and they won't hit on you. Oh, I was a naive little spirit.

James was locked down by the infamously temperamental Kristen Doute who, when I first met her, I liked. Her facial expressions always seemed friendly, even though, soon, her eyes would scream, *You're a ratchet whorebag.* Jax had bagged himself a sweet Southern belle named Brittany Cartwright, and when I heard about her, I asked Jax, "Tell me about this girlfriend of yours?"

"Easy with the word *girlfriend*," he replied, forgetting to mention that Brittany was somewhere halfway across America, with a car full of her belongings, hauling ass to LA to move in with him.

Sweet little Kentucky muffin, America's sweetheart—Brittany never wanted to be famous. She would have been perfectly content living in Kentucky, getting married, and having a family. But God had other plans for this Christian woman, who definitely wasn't a Lala fan when she arrived in Los Angeles—how could she be, when all she kept hearing was that "this whore is hitting on Jax and doesn't care he has a girlfriend?" I would have hated me, too.

One night at SUR, Carter booty-texted me. Because I was wasted and horny from all the flirting with Jax, I let him come and pick me up. That night, Carter and I had quite the night in bed. A night that pushed boundaries, took things to the next level. Yes, I ate his asshole, and later, I confided in James about it. Off camera, of course. I never thought for one tiny second that James would immediately blab about my sexual experiences on camera. But he did.

I found out when Faith gave me the heads-up, right before I was due to go to Hawaii with the rest of the cast. I had to tell Carter—that was the right thing to do—so I texted him explaining that "some stuff about our relationship" might get mentioned on the show. I didn't go into too much detail, figuring he wouldn't care too much. Wrong again. He was furious.

"I just want to play football, La! Don't *ever* talk about me on your damn show!"

After the extra intimate night we'd just had, it really hurt. Yet again, he was making me feel worthless, unloved, and uncared for. His words shook the feelings of confidence and control I'd managed to build up, and I found myself right back in the pit of shame and self-loathing I'd worked so hard to pull myself out of. *Fuck.*

Meanwhile, the girls at SUR were getting meaner and more vicious by the day. *Lala's a slut, a whore, a hooker, a gold digger who gives BJs on Italian yachts for money.* . . . It didn't seem to matter how nice I was to those girls, they seemed hell-bent on painting me as some scarlet woman of the night. My Instagram profile pic combined with my "suspicious" trip to Italy was proof enough to them that I was a hooker—although, excuse me, if I actually was hooking, do you really think I'd be hostessing at a goddamn restaurant instead of shopping for designer bags and Louboutin stripper heels? The guys were fanning the flames of their bullshit gossip, saying that *I* was the one who had initiated the flirting with them. As if. *To hell with* all *of them,* I thought. *You think I'm a whore and a slut? I'll show you what a whore and a slut looks like! The more you ho-shame me, the more I'll talk about BJs around your dudes. I'll show you what slutty looks like. I'll shove it right down your throat!*

And that is how my top ended up coming off in Hawaii, in front of the entire male cast. Did I do this to get a rise? Yes and no. During this time of my life, Danielle and I couldn't go near a body of water without our tops coming off, and since this was a reality show, I needed to show what I *really* do when I'm on vacation. The girls reacted exactly as predicted and doubled down on their hate. The toxic cycle had commenced. The meaner they were to me, the wilder I became. I didn't care about anything or anyone, or what they thought about me anymore. Only Lisa had my back. She told the girls they should never go to Europe if they don't like nipples, because over there girls' boobs will be coming out in front of your man every day. And she said that to label me a whore for taking my top off was just ignorant. Her support helped me feel slightly less alone. 'Cause most of the time, I felt like a one-woman defense squad, at war with some all time basic B's.

Then I learned that Carter's manager had reached out to one of the *Vanderpump* producers, wanting to set up a meeting to see how to incorporate him onto the show. Apparently, Carter's NFL career wasn't going great, and his manager figured since Carter was already being talked about on *Vanderpump*, they might as well make the most of it. I was *livid*. Carter had crushed me after our last exchange, how dare he now try to leverage our relationship to better *his* career? Thankfully the meeting never happened.

Halfway through the season, Stassi Schroeder, the GOAT basic bitch, rejoined the cast to add her personal vanilla to the atmosphere. Stassi had a long reality history—her family was on season eight of *The Amazing Race* in 2005, then in 2008, she was on a short-lived reality series called *Queen Bees* before joining

Vanderpump. This chick was built for reality TV, and unlike me, she knew exactly what she was doing. The girl had already built an empire based on being flavorless—her brand was drenched in ranch dressing and pinot grigio—and I did not vibe with her at all at first, because of what I perceived to be a lack of spice. I stand corrected. Stassi has taught me there's a big difference between doing basic shit, which can be kind of fun—who doesn't secretly love a pumpkin spice latte?—and just being bland. Because Stassi does in fact have a lot of flavor, one I have grown to love with all my heart, but when I first met her, that flavor tasted a lot like Satan. Stassi, Kristen, and Katie became the worst mean-girl trio ever, and it was three against one at all times. Thank the Lord for alcohol, the only thing that helped me get through each day with those girls.

Didn't matter where we were, or how formal the event, so long as I was hammered, I could handle whatever they threw at me. At Katie and Tom Schwartz's engagement party at Lisa Vanderpump's house, I got bored during Kristen and Stassi's long, pointless speech. *Fuck it,* I thought, not caring about these people or their lives.

"Can we wrap it up?" I yelled. "What the fuck are you talking about?" I was four cocktails and three shots deep, and my delivery didn't go down well in front of people's parents, including elderly family members who had flown in for this party. Katie was so mad, she took the mic away from Kristen and said something like if some people who were at the bottom of the guest list weren't happy, they could walk out the way they came in. I rolled my eyes and sucked down on my cocktail. Lala did not GAF. Lala was there to fuck shit up.

As soon as my first season started airing on Bravo, people started to recognize me in the street, and every episode that aired made me more of a "somebody." I saw my follower numbers rocket, alongside my confidence—it seemed like people were actually fans of "Lala," this drunk, somewhat insane person I had become in order to survive the assholes at SUR who hated me. Strange but true.

Everything was smoking and moving in an upward direction, and when I heard that James and I had been invited to guest on *Watch What Happens Live*, it felt like I had truly *arrived*. WWHL is the talk show hosted by Andy Cohen, daddy of Bravo and executive producer of some of the most popular reality formats ever. Everyone loves the show—I mean, he's had Meryl Streep and Cher on there as guests. And now, me and James.

Holy shit, I thought. *This is it. The dream.*

James and I were peas in a pod. I loved his Euro-LA swag, and I told him early on in our friendship, "When I get married, you will be my man of honor." We did everything together, and for a while I couldn't imagine my life without him in it. He always had my back (except for when he was blabbing secrets about my sex life to the rest of the cast), always made me laugh, and he was the best drinking buddy a girl could hope for. We'd make out on occasion, and although we never dated, we'd get jealous when the other person hooked up with someone else. Our friendship was a mind-fuck out the gate, but that's what made it special. Those were our glory days, on season four.

WWHL is filmed in New York, so Bravo booked us on an early flight from LAX to JFK. To James and me, a morning flight is the perfect occasion to start poppin' bottles, so we landed in New York three sheets to the wind with just enough time to get to the hotel, continue drinking, get glammed, and rush to the *WWHL* studio by 10:00 p.m. for a live taping at 11:00 p.m.

We arrived at the studio, and when I saw the cupcakes with our faces on them in the green room, I felt so dope. I couldn't believe someone had actually pulled pictures of my face from the Internet to put on a cupcake.

"We are so legit, James," I said, holding one up.

We sat in our seats opposite Andy and the show began. *WWHL* is only thirty minutes long, including commercials, and the vibe is 100 percent party. That goes for the viewers, too—they are given a "word of the night," and every time they hear it, they're supposed to have a drink. The guests are encouraged to get loose, too, and every break, someone refreshes your cocktail. They might have held off on the refills had they known how hammered James and I already were, and how loose we were about to get with our tongues.

"Guys, you can't curse," Andy said, the first time one of us let drop an f-bomb.

Then we did it again. Andy was getting pissed.

"Seriously you cannot curse on the show, stop."

I didn't realize that every time you say a curse word on live TV, they have to block out the sentence before and the sentence after. Because we were cursing so much, it seemed like the whole episode was on mute. Then we did it again, and Andy lost it.

"Is there any way you could stop cussing? I swear to God. You're driving me nuts. I'm not kidding."

His tone kind of scared me, so I told myself, *All right, no more cursing. Be good, Lala, be good.*

Then came the section of the show where they read out the tweets. Jax had of course tweeted something rude at us, about this being the most boring episode of *WWHL* he had ever seen—Jax is quick with the thumbs on Twitter and doesn't think about what he is saying. I looked dead straight into the camera and suggested that Jax think before he tweet, unless he wanted me to spill his deepest, ugliest secrets on live TV. And it only got worse from there.

At the end of every show, Andy Cohen gives out a Mazel of the Week, and a Jackhole of the Week. For example, the Mazel may go to Oprah for providing 100,000 meals to Feeding America and the Jackhole may go to Donald Trump because, well, he's being Donald Trump. That night, the Jackholes were James and myself.

James Kennedy and Lala Kent, the first guests in the history of *WWHL* to ever to receive the Jackhole.

After we finished taping the show, we expected Andy Cohen to take pictures with us for the step and repeat like he does with all his guests. But he exited the stage quickly, wanting no part of us. I didn't realize he was mad; as far as I was concerned, James and I had done great. We were super entertaining, we were rock stars. James and I wound up taking our own pictures in front of the Bravo *Watch What Happens Live* sign, on cloud nine.

As we walked out of the building, a young man was out there, waiting for me, with his mom. He said he was a big fan of mine and asked if he could take a photo. He was tall and thin, with dark hair, facial scruff, and had a sweet spirit about him. All I could think was *Holy shit. He's a fan. A real fan! Of me. How is this even happening?* This shit was going to my head, and I have to say, it was very satisfying. I was getting known, I was being recognized in the street, my Instagram following was through the roof—I had close to 300,000 followers now! People wanted more of this person they were seeing on TV, and who was I to deprive them of their wishes?

Give the people what they want, I thought. *Give them Lala.*

His mom took a picture of us, then showed me for approval. I was wearing my emerald-green dress, spaghetti straps, and my eyes were bloodshot from the alcohol I'd been guzzling since morning. Even worse, I had a shiny, greasy face—you could tell: that girl is living her best life.

"Thanks, Lala," he said, after taking the picture. "See you next time."

We got back to the hotel around 4:00 a.m., and I was so drunk, I couldn't have gotten any drunker. Nonetheless, I felt anxious and couldn't sleep. I tossed and turned until the sun came up, and when it did, I grabbed my phone and immediately googled myself, a weird feeling in my stomach.

The whole world was talking about how awful Lala Kent and James Kennedy were, and Andy was saying how disappointed he was in us. I was mortified, embarrassed, devastated. I couldn't believe I had acted such a fool. I come from an amazing family, I had an incredible upbringing; why had I allowed myself to act that way?

I called my dad, Kent, as soon as I knew he'd be awake and told him everything. He and my mom had never watched *Vanderpump Rules*, or *WWHL* (to this day, my mom hasn't seen an episode of *Vanderpump*), so I gave him a play-by-play of what had happened, the ugly truth of how their daughter had behaved, white girl wasted on live TV.

"Lauren, I want you to forgive yourself," he said. "People make mistakes. Tomorrow, someone more famous will do something stupid, and everyone will be talking about that instead. Talk to the people from the show and apologize. Be honest. Tell them you got excited, and had too much to drink. It'll be okay."

I wanted so badly to hug my dad for always being the sweetest, kindest person I knew, and for always giving me the advice I needed to hear.

I called one of the producers of *Vanderpump Rules*, and he suggested that an email to Lisa Vanderpump and Andy Cohen might be a nice gesture, so I wrote a heartfelt note to them both. Lisa immediately forgave me—honestly, God bless that woman, I am so grateful for her—but Andy was still very upset, and I wasn't sure he'd ever warm back up to me. From feeling like I was winning, I was now starting to feel like the world's biggest jackass.

Not long afterward, Carter saw the episode where James talked about the intimate details of our sex life that I had shared with him. Oh boy . . . I had tried to forget about that, and really hoped no one would ever notice, but that's not how life works on reality TV. EVERYONE noticed, including all of Carter's friends who happened to watch the episode. I felt sick as the barrage of furious text messages rolled in from Carter.

"My boys are telling me what's being said," he wrote me. "I can't believe you would do this to me!" And on and on. This time, I couldn't even get mad at him for yelling at me. I tried to calm him down, but he wouldn't respond. He just shut me down. Left me in the dust. I'd worked so hard to believe I was someone—and I was, I had done what I set out to do: I had 300,000 followers on the 'gram. But mentally, Carter had put me right back in my place. He made me feel like I was nothing. A joke.

By the time it came to filming the season four reunion, I was a mess of emotions. I didn't drink for that taping, because I knew Andy was hosting the reunion, and I didn't want to do or say anything stupid again. I knew I could do better, so I tried really hard to be more Lauren, the version of myself that is sweet, polite, and in control. Andy saw a different, more subdued side of me, and I think he must have realized that I wasn't a monster after all. Lala has many different sides to her, and walking away from the reunion, I felt excited about unleashing her again the following season. I couldn't wait to see what she had in store. . . .

chapter three

"I, LAUREN BURNINGHAM, WILL NOT STOP UNTIL I AM IN THE MOVIES."

heathen (noun)

hea·then /hēTHən

an uncivilized or irreligious person

*O*NCE UPON A TIME, the founding fathers of Mormonism arrived in Utah and said, "This is the place," and from that point on, Utah was dominated by the Mormon faith, with very little separation between church and state—I mean, how could there be, when the Church of Jesus Christ of Latter-day Saints is worth $100 billion? They own everything in Utah, and if you own it, you run it.

When people in LA learn I grew up in Utah, sometimes they ask how many moms I have, which is ridiculous. So let me fill you in: there are two branches of Mormonism—Latter-day Saints (LDS) and the Fundamentalist Latter-day Saints (FLDS). LDS is a regular religion, and FLDS has a history of polygamy. Polygamy is now illegal in the state of Utah, and the sister wives and their husbands now mainly live in Arizona, Nevada, and Colorado. That doesn't mean you won't see one of these cult-loving, brainwashed little humans bopping around my home state, if you look hard enough.

If you're a regular true-blue Mormon, you pay your 10 percent tithing, go to temple, and wear the "holy underwear" that goes underneath your sexy bra and underwear. Holy underwear is long and prevents women from showing too much skin around their chest, shoulders, and above the knee. Which all sounds very conservative, but bear in mind that Salt Lake City also has one of the largest gay pride parades in the nation, with a giant float for the Mormon moms of gay and lesbian children, and Utah was one of the first states to legalize gay marriage. So, it's a complex, unusual mix of people and attitudes, with intolerance and acceptance living side by side.

One thing's for sure, though; if you're Mormon, you're living a rule-filled life. You don't drink coffee or tea because caffeine is banned (although they love to down Diet Coke like it's water . . . riddle me that one). Absolutely no alcohol or drugs are allowed—unless you're prescribed something, which many of them are, to deal with the anxiety and depression that comes from being part of a guilt-based religion. If Mormons are good at one thing, it's judging. Themselves, and others. I know a lot of people who left the Church for that reason. They couldn't handle the pressure, and who can blame them?

My dad left the Church when he was twenty-two. There were too many things the Church was telling him not to do, too many hard-and-fast ideas on what made you a bad person, none of which resonated with him. That's why, even though I grew up in Salt Lake, I was never, ever involved in Mormon practice. My brother and I were raised to be spiritual, without any specific religious denomination in mind. We were taught that you don't need a book to teach you how to love and accept; all you need is a working mind and heart.

Because my dad had turned his back on Mormonism, his family looked at us as outsiders who were living in sin. In their eyes, anybody who didn't practice what they practiced needed to be rescued. My uncle, who was a Mormon bishop, tried his best to lure me into the Church once by saying, "I have a lot of good-looking Polynesians in the priesthood right now." Utah has a sizable Tongan and Samoan population, and all the guys on my high school football team were super-hot Polynesians built like Jason Momoa.

"Yes, please do send them my way," I said.

"No, Lauren. The only way I'll introduce you is if you start going to church every Sunday."

"Eh, keep 'em. That's not happening."

The Mormon side of my family would gather once a month for Grandma Mary-Lynn's big Sunday dinner. Mary-Lynn, my dad's mom, was your typical American grandma—super cute and plump, gave the best hugs, and her house always smelled like she was baking cookies and scones—to this day, those are the best scones I've ever had. Her home was decorated in floral prints and filled with lots of musical instruments, because she played the piano and violin. She was a schoolteacher who single-handedly taught my brother and me how to read and write and do math, more so than my teachers at school, and she gave us Nestle's pink milk while we did our homework. But, like the rest of my dad's family, she was very, very Mormon, balls-deep in the Church. Mormonism wasn't just her religion, it was her life.

My mom sometimes skipped Mary-Lynn's monthly dinners, but I kept going because I kind of enjoyed the quiet, uptight awkwardness of it all. When I was around seventeen, we were at Grandma's for Sunday dinner, and I casually mentioned that I was going to my boyfriend's house afterward for sexy time, just to see how they'd react. It was always easy to provoke a reaction from this group of people, and I do love to entertain. Thanks to my darling Mormon family, I learned how to shock a room of very nice, conservative Americans right out of their holy underwear, because it's fun. A skill that would be useful to me, later on in my reality TV career.

My mom didn't play the "let's piss off a Mormon" game like I did; thank God. It would have been weird if she'd rolled up to

Grandma's in a miniskirt and talked about sexy time, like I did, just to remind everyone that we were different, and *we won't conform*. When I told her about my little stunt, she laughed and told me I was a little heathen. I now have the word *heathen* tattooed above my elbow on my left arm. Was I intoxicated when I chose to do so? Heavily. But I have no regrets. It's still one of my favorite tattoos.

Contrary to what my dad's side of the family might think, I actually do respect God. I like feeling that he has my back, and he loves me whether I am acting like a damn fool or not. But Mormonism? No, thank you—I refuse to be controlled to that degree. From childhood, I had no interest in rules. I wanted to live, be free, and, above all, perform. This little heathen was a big old drama queen, from birth, as you may have already guessed.

Even though I've mellowed in my thirty years, I'm still often told by my family and fiancé that I'm a little dramatic. Everything is a big to-do, because drama is all I've ever known. As a kid, I was a jokester and a class clown who craved a grand, emotional moment above all else. Like when, at the ripe old age of seven, I pranced into my mom's bathroom to deliver some big, earth-shattering news. Mom was in the bathtub, reading a magazine.

"Mom, I want to be an actress," I announced, thinking, *One day, my mom will be on* E! True Hollywood Story, *crying, as she describes this incredible moment.*

I thought my mom would throw her magazine down, jump out

of the bath with tears in her eyes, and say "That is so amazing, Lauren! I'm so proud! I know you're going to make it!"

But all I got was a glance, a smile, and the words, "Aw. That is so sweet!"

Then she got back to her magazine, somehow unaware of the moment's gravitas.

Mary-Kate and Ashley Olsen—they were a big part of why I wanted to act. I watched every TV show and movie they made, read every book they published. I wanted to play pretend like they did: on *Full House* where they were part of a huge family with lots of kids, and on *Our Lips Are Sealed*, where they witnessed a crime and were put into a witness-protection program with their family. I remember thinking it must be so fun to spend your days getting to be someone who isn't you. And as soon as I figured out there was a word for that—*acting*—it seemed obvious that's what I should do with the rest of my life.

I was on a playdate with my childhood friend Candice one afternoon, sharing my hopes and dreams for a show-business future, when her mom, Kristin, presented me with a little note card that read:

I, Lauren Burningham, will not stop until I am in the movies.

Below was an X and a line for a signature.

"Okay, Lauren, what this means is you'll have to always work hard to succeed at your dream."

"Okay," I said. "I'll sign it right now!"

I had no problem signing this sweet little card with its declaration that I was now contractually bound to.

A few years later, it was time to get this dream on the road. I enrolled in my very first acting class with Josh Stevens, a local acting coach who was also a casting director for Disney movies shot in Utah. I had high hopes that if I was a familiar face in his class, I'd have a better chance of booking the films he was casting for. I was a determined and ambitious little drama queen; I suppose I still am.

Little divas tend to be very sensitive, though, and for me that led to anxiety, something I still contend with today. I was an old soul, with complicated emotions that sometimes overwhelmed me. After a hard day at elementary school, I would sit on the couch in front of the TV, feeling incredibly guilty that I wasn't out working, earning my keep, doing more to help my family. I was a feeler and an overthinker, and my mind often went to some very grown-up places for such a young kid.

Sometimes I would get upset over minor things that had nothing to do with me—if I saw an older person eating by themselves, for example, the sadness would be crushing. I would assume they were all alone in the world, with nobody who loved them enough to eat with them. My mom would have to gently explain, "Lauren, they probably chose to go out to have lunch by themselves and read a book. It's nice to be alone. Sometimes when you lose yourself, you find yourself." What she meant by that was, that sometimes you need to get out of your head so you can remember that life is good and know that not everything needs to be solved. Big lessons for a kid to learn; I'm still working on them to this day.

After school, most of my friends would go home and watch Disney shows. My tastes, however, leaned toward adult pop culture and gossip, and *E! News* and *106 & Park* on BET were my jam. I loved how celebrities were quoted on issues of the day—which made me realize that being an actress wasn't about just entertaining people, or the paycheck you make, or the fame that comes along with it. It's much bigger than that. People in the public eye have a job to do off the screen and off the stage, too, and that job is to use their voices to make a difference.

The first day of seventh grade, I walked into my sixth-period woodworking class with Mr. Wallace with that in mind. I never became much of a woodworker, but what came out of that class stays engraved in my mind to this day. Mr. Wallace gave us each a piece of paper and asked us to write down what we wanted to be when we were older. I still wanted to be in movies, but now there was more to it than that. My goals had shifted, slightly, seven years on. This time, my answer was: I, Lauren Burningham, want to be a role model.

I had moved on from Mary-Kate and Ashley and found some grown-up role models who really used their voices to make change in the world. Beyoncé was one. I loved her music, her style, her strength as a woman. Kobe Bryant, I was obsessed with. Not only was he an amazing basketball player, but he also lived his life with purpose and had a powerful message. They became my go-to role models from the world of celebrity. But the people who taught me most were my mom and my dad, my makers, Mr. and Mrs. Burningham. They never judged me, so I never judged myself, or others. They never made me frightened of telling the truth, which meant I was able do the same on national television. From them, I have learned everything I need to know about self-acceptance, courage, and, most of all, love. They're up there with Bey and Kobe, as far as I'm concerned.

Lisa, my mom, was nineteen and working at a department store called Castletons in Salt Lake City when a handsome fella with a killer mustache and gold chain necklace approached her—his name was Kent Burningham, and he was a young businessman running a real-estate development company. Kent would come in often to shop for clothing that he probably didn't even need, just so he could wait for Lisa to be available to scan his items and check him out. Literally and figuratively.

After a handful of these encounters, Kent plucked up the courage to ask my mom on a date. During this time, Lisa was dating other dudes who, no shock at all, didn't compare to Kent. She ditched the clowns and became exclusive with Kent. They had a standing date night on Thursdays and Saturdays. Like all relationships, there were bumps in the road, and Lisa would catch an attitude at times, but Kent would respond by showering her with love that she may not have deserved in the moment, but that fixed every-thing. Love was my dad's secret weapon—he had a lot of it to give, and it always worked like a charm. Hearing about my parents' early years together reminds me of my relationship with my fiancé, Randall. Like Rand and I, my mom and dad were lovers and best friends, ride-or-dies.

Lisa and Kent had different upbringings: Lisa was born into a Christian family in Texas; her mom was a Southern belle from Georgia, and her dad was in the army, so they moved around a lot before settling down in Utah. Kent was Utah-born and raised, one of four kids from a strict Mormon family, where religion played a huge part of their upbringing. Kent had been married once, to a Mormon woman with whom he had one son; my older brother, Brandon. (Some people correct me with that "half brother" non-sense, but to me, Brandon is my brother, period.) Kent was young when he split from his first wife, around twenty-two, and they got a "temple divorce" on top of the regular legal divorce. A temple di-vorce means that when you die, you're not stuck with your ex in the afterlife. Afterward, both my dad and his ex-wife exited the Church completely and crossed over to the fun side of life, luckily for me.

Kent and Lisa dated for seven years before he finally popped the question at his family's condo in St. George, Utah, about an hour out of Zion National Park. They were engaged for a year be-fore tying the knot. When I ask my mom why she allowed him to take that long to propose, her answer is "I never even thought about it!" We are very different in that way—my mom likes to go with the flow, live in the moment, and views life like a hurdle race; if you look up to see how many hurdles you have left, you'll trip and fall, so it's better to just keep your head down and jump one after the other. I'm the opposite—always looking ten hurdles ahead.

After a year's engagement, they married, and not long afterward, on September 2, 1990, I, Lauren Burningham, sign of the Virgo, finally arrived on this earth. My dad had been working hard to finish building our house in Olympus Cove to bring me home to. Olympus Cove is a neighborhood on the slopes of Mount Olympus, on the east side of Salt Lake City, and our house was tucked in a cul-de-sac, with a direct view of the mountain. It was a mile away from my school; half a mile to the strip mall that had a grocery store and Hollywood Video, where all the neighborhood kids would go; and walking distance to my grandparents' house. My dad, mom, little brother, Easton, and I all lived there together for twenty-three years, until I relocated to LA. My mom still lives in that house today.

During the nineties, my dad's real-estate business started blowing up. He was building ten- to fifteen-million-dollar houses, and making bank. I remember going to his amazing office and thinking it was so cool that my dad was such a boss. I would watch him on the phone, closing deals, just being such a badass.

We never wanted for anything, but I was not a spoiled kid. In fact, once I was past a certain age, I had to work for everything. When I was seven, I remember desperately wanting the DVD of Rodgers and Hammerstein's *Cinderella*, starring Whitney Houston and Brandy. My mom said I had to earn money to pay for it by doing chores. I was furious—I thought she should go to Hollywood Video the next day and bring it home for me. When she didn't, I got so mad, I hit her. That got me grounded for the first time. Lesson learned.

Afterward, Mom explained the rules to me. Cleaning my own room did not count as a chore because "I shouldn't have to compensate you for keeping your own room clean." Instead, I could vacuum the stairs, make her bed, go outside and weed, or plant flowers. Any of those tasks would earn me some money. Eventually, I did enough chores to earn the money for the *Cinderella* DVD. And when I decided I wanted the Spice Girls watch from Fred Meyer hypermarkets (it was white, had the Spice Girls' faces inside it, and cost $25), I had to chore super hard in order to buy it. My parents were instilling in me a work ethic, something I'm very grateful for to this day.

The only time we didn't have to work for toys was on birthdays and at Christmas. That's when we got whatever the hell we wanted. In fact, my brother Easton and I never once doubted that Santa Claus was real because we always got *exactly* what we'd asked for on our list, to the letter. I always asked for a Lee Middleton baby doll, these dolls that are so realistic you can even order "premature" ones. We had a Lee Middleton store in Salt Lake and it was, like, my heaven. I asked for one every Christmas, and I always got it, with the exact baby clothes I had picked out for it. Not doll's clothes—*actual baby clothes* that I had selected from a babywear catalog. This is how obsessive and detail-oriented I was with fashion, even from a young age. Everything had to be exactly right, and I took care of those dolls like they were real babies.

My entire life, I saw my mom go to work, even though she didn't need to because my dad's business was doing so well. My mama taught me to save, to take care of my possessions, to work hard, and to never depend on a man. Never share a bank account, and keep everything separate in case one day he leaves, or God forbid, he finds himself in hot water with the big dick of the law and they try to snatch all of your possessions. Mom worked at an orthodontist's office, she taught special needs kids, and then she got a job at the Humane Society of Utah, where she still works today. She worked her ass off, always, saving money just in case one day we had to kick into survival mode. Thank goodness she did.

My mom usually went to work early, before my dad, so it was up to my dad to get Easton and me ready for school—there was no such thing as gender roles in my house. Dad would blow-dry my hair and always gave me the most epic curled bangs, we call it the Utah claw, rock-solid from all the hair spray. He was so stellar, so hands-on, and participated equally in housework; he would do all the ironing, and his side of the bathroom would be pristine, whereas my mom's would look like a bomb went off.

Weekday mornings were usually fun at our house—the TV was always turned on, drapes and blinds would be open; it was always lively when Dad woke us up for school. One morning, though, things felt different. My little brother, Easton, and I were awakened by my mom, who seemed in a hurry and stressed. The drapes were still closed in her bedroom, the TV was off, and my dad was lying in bed in the fetal position.

"What's wrong with Dad?" I asked.

"He's just not feeling very good," my mom said. "I'm going to take you to school, then come back to take him to the doctor."

My eight-year-old mind was racing. I was worried. I said a prayer on my way to school, because my dad was big on prayers. Not the culty Mormon kind, just spiritual ones he would say every night with Easton and me before bed. They always made me feel at ease. In the car, I asked God to take care of my dad and prayed he would be okay. I finished the prayer with "In your precious name I pray, amen."

We arrived at Eastwood Elementary; I got out of the car and headed into class. When the bell rang at 3:00 p.m., my brother and I walked up the giant hill to the crosswalk, where, like many other students, we always got picked up from school. I didn't see my mom's car, which wasn't a big deal; she never left us waiting for more than a few minutes if she was ever late.

Easton and I waited and waited. After all the kids had been picked up except us, the crossing guard, a sweet old man who had been volunteering for that job since before I was a student there, asked me if I wanted to call my mom. I did, but there was no answer, so I decided to walk home with my six-year-old little brother. It was a safe neighborhood where everybody knew everybody, and the walk was less than a mile. Still, though, something didn't feel right.

We made it home, I made both of us a snack, and I took care of Easton while we were home alone. I locked all the doors and took him to the playroom, where I could entertain him and try to keep my mind off the fact that I didn't know where my parents were. Less than an hour after we got home, a white Lexus pulled into the driveway. It was my aunt Laura, my dad's sister. I was so happy to see her! She told us that everything was okay and she was taking us to Brenda's house to play with our cousins. Brenda was my dad's other sister.

My aunt Laura dropped us off at our cousins' house and got back in her car, rushing off. By this point, I *knew* something was wrong. I wasn't the kind of kid you could stick in front of some Barbies and I'd be good. I faked my smile and laughter while fixating on my aunt Brenda's energy. I watched her every move. The phone rang, and she went outside in the front yard to talk. This was back when people had landlines, and if you picked up the phone while someone else was on it, you could eavesdrop. So I did. I heard Aunt Brenda on the phone with Aunt Laura.

"Brenda, you need to get the kids here. This could very well be the last time they see him."

My heart raced as I put the phone down, just as my aunt Brenda ran into the house.

"Kids, we're going to meet your mom and Aunt Laura and Uncle Roger at the hospital to see your dad." Her voice trembled. She was trying to look positive, but I could see it in her eyes. Fear.

We rushed to the hospital, and my brother and I were led into my dad's hospital room. I saw a slice from his chest bone to just above his belly button, which had been stapled shut. He had a giant tube in his stomach, just below the incision. He was unconscious, still sedated from his surgery.

I asked what was happening. Someone said his heart valve had gone out, the part of the body that controls how much blood gets to your heart. His heart was being flooded. My dad had been minutes away from dying, and these surgeons, who will forever be my angels, performed emergency open-heart surgery and saved my dad's life. My dad had gotten a titanium valve put in his heart and was told he had to be on blood thinners for the rest of his life. But he was alive. They saved him, and soon after, he was able to come home.

I remember his titanium valve. It would make a soft ticking

sound, like a clock. It brought me so much comfort when I was next to him, hearing that tick, because I knew it meant his heart was working. Sometimes, though, it felt like a reminder of the moments ticking away from my father's life. I tried my best not to think about it that way.

My mom told me a few years later that the doctor she had originally taken my dad to that day—let's call him Dr. Raymus because it rhymes with *anus*—sent him home, saying, "Nothing's wrong." My mom, thankfully, knew better, and took him to the hospital, where the surgeons told her that if she had waited another hour, he would have died. I went to school with the first doctor's daughter, and every time I saw her I wanted to sucker punch her in the face and scream, "YOUR DAD ALMOST KILLED MY DAD!"

Not long after his heart procedure, my dad suffered more health problems and had to have a colonoscopy. It was supposed to be a simple procedure, in and out in a day. But a nurse called us from the hospital saying there was an emergency and we needed to come immediately. We rushed into his room, and I remember being shocked by the sight of blood splattered all over the walls. Because of the blood thinners he was taking, he was bleeding internally, and it became a life-or-death situation. Thankfully, he survived. Then, not too long after that, he cut his tongue on a gingersnap cookie and almost bled to death. Again, it was because of the blood thinners. Hundreds of thousands of people are put on blood thinners every single day and they live normal, carefree lives, but we could never seem to find the right levels with my dad.

My dad was such a strong man and so successful in many ways, the toughest person I think I've ever met in my life. But after those health scares, my dad became, to me, like the Bubble Boy. From the time I was eight, nothing was normal, because something as harmless as a cookie could turn into a life-or-death situation. Most people look back at their childhood and they think, *My dad could have been nicer*, or *My mom could have been less hard on me*. My childhood was a dream, but I was constantly in fear of losing my dad.

From the age of eight, I understood that each day with my father was precious because it could also be his last. Already a sensitive kid, I started to experience anxiety on a level that most eight-year-olds probably don't, because every time I looked at him I'd wonder about his heart and if it was beating. My life was perfect, free and filled with love—but I could never escape the worry that it could all be gone the next day.

chapter four

BOSSING UP TO BULLIES

BACKSTABBING, BULLIES, AND DEATH threats—I'm not talking about *Vanderpump Rules*, I'm talking about motherfucking elementary school.

I was nine years old when I received my first online death threat. I had one of those Apple computers that looked like a bubble TV and came in different colors. Mine was blue. I got home from school, fired that bad boy up, waited for my dial-tone Internet to kick in, and launched AOL Instant Messenger. In the chat room, I saw a message:

I'm going to kill you one day.

It was sent by this granola kid, Phillip, who was in my third-grade homeroom class. I can't remember exactly what I wrote back to him, but it was definitely a lyric from a Tupac song. This threat came shortly after the horrific Columbine shooting, so when I showed my mom, she lost it. She called Principal Hicks and demanded he bring Phillip and his mom into the school for a meeting between us all. Principal Hicks agreed.

Phillip rolled in with his mom, and I could see why he was a hippie type of kid—his mom had long gray hair and wore Patagonia and Tevas. She looked super zen and cool. We started the meeting, and Principal Hicks asked about the message. Phillip was staring at his hands, looking embarrassed.

"Phillip, what made you send that message to Lauren?" Principal Hicks asked.

Finally, Phillip spoke.

"In class, we were sitting down for reading and someone farted and my friend told me Lauren blamed it on me!"

Little fucking Phillip. My mom looked like her head had just exploded.

"My child is receiving death threats over a *fart*? This is absolutely not okay!" My mom went Turbo Karen on them, and rightfully so. See, this wasn't the first time I'd been singled out by bullies, and it wouldn't be the last. I guess there's just something about me that haters seem to love. . . .

Kids at my school were constantly blaming me for things I never did. Poking fun at me. When it was happening, I didn't recognize it as bullying. Sure, I'd hear my mom say the word *bully*. On the phone with her mom, my grandma Mimi, I heard her crying, saying, "I just want my baby girl happy. She's having a tough little time at school." But when it's happening to you every day, it seems normal; just another day in the schoolyard.

In fourth grade, I wanted to be in class with Mr. Cushner, a teacher who everyone loved. All my best girlfriends were in that class, but I'd been put with Ms. Tremont, who I thought was kind of scary. I asked my mom if she could go into school and get me switched into Mr. Cushner's class, so I could be with my friends, but when she came home from her meeting with Mr. Miller, she walked in the door in tears.

"Mom, what's wrong?"

"Mr. Cushner doesn't want you in his class because he says that you referred to him as a 'fat retard.' Is that true, Lauren?"

I had never said that. *Never*. Apparently, one of my "friends" had told Mr. Cushner that lie, one of the girls I had wanted to be in class with, in fact. I thought we were friends. I realized then that we weren't. I ended up staying in Ms. Tremont's class, and I loved her. She was a champion. And I didn't hang out much with my "girlfriends" much after that. Seemed like some of them were just . . . mean.

My mom could see how stressed out I was. No matter how

many conversations she had with the principal, school was becoming a place of daily conflict for me. One afternoon, when I came home furious again because of what some kid had said to me, she took my cheeks in her hands and said, "I have an idea, let's go to LA. Take your mind off things."

She booked us a room at a cute boutique hotel on Wilshire Boulevard. I remember feeling like the city was so big and so full of life, it made the mean girls at school seem less important, somehow. We would drive through the neighborhoods, from Echo Park to Beverly Hills, and I'd soak it all up. LA wasn't a small bubble like Salt Lake. Here, everyone was different. I wanted those times to last forever. Just me and my mama bear. I felt safe, I felt happy.

Mom took me to a salon to get highlights put in my hair and acrylic nails. Was it normal for a fourth grader to have highlights and nails? Hell no. But my mom did what she had to do to make me feel like I was special, and she did. When the time came for us to leave, I stood outside on the balcony of our hotel room and told California, "I'm going to come back. I'm going to live here one day. There's going to be a time where I never leave you."

My mental state really improved after that trip to LA, so the next time I started feeling down about what was happening at school, my mom took me back. The same thing happened in junior high. Whenever I was bullied, whenever things got really bad, my mom would whisk me to LA for a time-out. Today, the truancy court system would probably have come after us, but my homework was always done, and I was a beast with that extra credit. After these little vacays, I felt like I could go back to the schoolyard and tear shit up if I had to. My mom would shower me with words that made me feel like a champion, and because of what she did for me as a kid, I'm able to walk this earth feeling like I'm a five-star bitch.

Yes, I loved getting my hair and nails done, but growing up I was more sporty than girly; in fact, I was a Kobe Bryant–obsessed, basketball-hooping, softball-batting, soccer-ball-kicking tomboy. And when my mom laid out my outfits every night for school the next day, I would throw the outfit she chose in the laundry basket (to make it look like I wore it) and wear my basketball shorts, basketball shoes, and sweatshirt instead.

Because I was five foot six at the age of eleven, I kicked ass at basketball. I always pictured my hero, Kobe Bryant, when I would play. In one of my highest-scoring games, I made eighty points. This, for some reason, rubbed my teammates the wrong way, because the next time I played, the other girls on the team did not pass me the ball at all. I'd be wide open on the court, and they wouldn't pass me the ball. This became a regular thing. After the game, no one would come find me to take the group picture, or they'd push me to the end and make it look like I wasn't a part of the team. Our games were on Saturdays, and then Mondays at school the girls would all hang out, my little basketball team, but make damn sure that they did not speak to me. I didn't understand what I was doing wrong. I was on sports teams with these girls, we went to after-school programs together. Often, I would hang out with those same girls one-on-one on the weekends, then the following day at school, they would ignore me. It didn't make sense.

One Sunday, a really popular girl named Rosie was at my house watching *Little Nicky*, an Adam Sandler movie, with me. We were having a really nice time, but I felt sick to my stomach because the next day was Monday, and I knew what that meant. Monday was when I didn't have any friends anymore.

I looked at her and said, "Rosie, I really, really hate when I'm hanging out with my friends on the weekends and then the next day they don't talk to me. It hurts my feelings."

"Yeah," she said. "That sounds awful."

The next day, I hoped she'd be nice, considering our conversation, but she wasn't. It was the same shit. Every day, I wondered why. It couldn't be because I wasn't Mormon; a lot of those kids weren't Mormon. I knew I was a little different—most of the girls listened to Britney Spears, and I was into Tupac and the Geto Boys—but music taste alone didn't seem like reason enough to hate me. After a while I gave up trying to understand. If the girls didn't want to hang with me, I'd just play basketball with the boys during recess instead. Then I'd go back to the classroom and keep my head down, until the school day was over.

Countless children are bullied every day, and I was one of them. I learned enough about the bully mind-set to know I couldn't change them, because I don't think bullies are smart enough to even know what they are doing. But I did know that I could change my own mind-set. I reprogrammed my brain. I went toes with them, and my mouth was my weapon. That was how I fought. I would never put my hands on anyone, but I developed a very sharp, quick tongue because it was the only way I could stick up for myself. My self-defense mechanism was *I'm going to slaughter you with my words to the point where you're never going to want to talk to me again*, and it worked. Soon enough, people started leaving me alone. It got to the point where my mom would drop me off at school and instead of saying "Have a great day, honey!" she'd tell me "Be nice, Lauren!"

I'd shrug and say, "I'll try!"

Growing up in an affluent neighborhood on the east side of Salt Lake, I got used to being around a lot of very privileged people who lived in giant homes. I, too, had grown up very blessed, thanks to my dad's business success, but compared to a lot of my friends, my family's bank account was in the minor leagues.

I went to school with kids whose families balled out. I'm talking wealth; old money, billionaires. Like the Huntsmans, Mormons who own a petrochemicals company and, later, the *Salt Lake Tribune* newspaper. These people lived lives that were unfathomable. It was actually weird to see them stroll into school like they just came from the same house I did. I'd always wonder, if you're worth that much money, do you think about it? Do they look at their homes and go, "Holy shit, it's insane," or is it just home for them?

When I started at Skyline High School, you could see the wealth as you pulled into the parking lot on the first day of school, with kids driving their new Range Rover or the G-wagen they got for their sixteenth birthday. Girls would have on a new Tiffany bracelet, or a Louis Vuitton backpack. One dude cruised around in a Ferrari. He claimed it was his Ferrari, but I'm still convinced it was his dad's. Either way, I was impressed—I mean, I was ballin' out in my dad's Ford Expedition when I got my license. Picture baby Lala, sixteen years old, driving a tank like that. I whipped it around like it was a Fiat.

By high school, I had come into my own a bit. I'd bossed up, pulled myself together, and ditched my profound love for basketball shorts and sweatshirts. I was now the theater and choir chick with a push-up bra and killer cake-up. Even though my vibrato and highlights were poppin', I stayed to myself—I had PTSD from being bullied previous years, but to my relief, sophomore year was easy as pie. The senior girls were dope and took me under their wing, protecting me from the trolls in my grade who had been pushing my buttons since pre-K. But all good things must come to an end, and when my sophomore year came to a close, my girlfriends in the senior class moved on to greener pastures. I was back at square one, and people I'd never even talked to began to mess with me.

One time, I was at a bagel place for lunch when a kid from school walked up to me, poured coffee down my white shirt, and walked away. Afterward, I was too upset to go back to school, so I called my mom to come get me. She came and calmed me down, because I was hysterical, checked me out of school, and I followed her home, in my car.

We were about to pull into our circle when a car full of kids drove by, and one of them threw a Big Gulp of Pepsi on my windshield while yelling something. My mom, furious, hightailed it after them, and I followed in my car. There she was, a few blocks away, pulled over, talking to a bunch of random kids from school, tearing them a new asshole. I got out of my car and walked up to the kids.

"What have I ever done to you?" I asked one of the girls.

"Nothing," she said. "You've never done anything to me."

"So how can you feel like it's okay to bully me and throw shit at my car?"

No answer.

No one could give me a reason for why this was happening.

When I joined the cast of *Vanderpump Rules*, it felt exactly the same. Girls slut-shaming me and ganging up on me because maybe I was too extra, or because I challenged their ideas of how they thought a woman should behave.

"Do you realize I spent eighteen years of my life trying to get away from this shit?" I wanted to scream. Instead, I reverted back to my old tactics. Attack before you are attacked. And a couple cocktails sure helped.

The popular girls in my grade were all cheerleaders. I hate cheerleaders. I really do. I cannot stand that preppy bullshit. Also, they were mean—many times, I'd head to my car after school to find maxi pads all over it (thank goodness they were fresh, not used, but still it was kind of like being in *Carrie*); or I'd go to the lunchroom to collect my school pictures and they'd all be ripped up; they also did this to my school dance photos on more than one occasion. I knew exactly who was doing this to me—it was cheerleader Morgan Cutler and her minions. Morgan's Goody Two-shoes, little Mormon soul went on to get knocked up her senior year and was in and out of rehab after high school. Still, after all the bitchy things she did to me, I got her a baby gift. Hey, did I mention I hate cheerleaders?

In high school, there was one place I could escape the mean girls. Theater. That was my oasis. Theater was the place I could be the little weirdo I truly was. But the first time I walked into theater class, the other students looked at me like I must be mistaken. I wore short skirts and a lot of makeup and probably looked like the cheerleader type, but I really wasn't. I was a little eccentric. And more innocent than I dressed. The only penis I'd seen was the one in a maturation book. Once they realized I wasn't anything like what they thought, everyone warmed up to me and we became a tight little squad.

Some of the kids were nerds, some of the kids were gay but hadn't told their parents yet, and all of us were weirdos, in one way or another. I loved them all. Those were my people, and honestly, I wouldn't find another group who I considered "my people," again until eleven years later when I walked into my first AA meeting.

When my theater class kids told me they were being bullied, too, this made my blood boil. These sweet kids, a lot of whom were very sensitive, were being harassed? Oh, *hell* no. Abuse of my fellow weirdos was not going to be tolerated. Kristoff was super smart and really into digging in the dirt outdoors and looking at insects, and was being bullied by this other kid, Jack. Every day, Jack would call him names and mess with him at lunch. My mom knew Kristoff because he got his braces at the orthodontist practice where she worked. One day, Kristoff's mom called my mom and said, "Hey, Jack is giving Kristoff a really hard time at school. This has been going on since junior high. Do you think Lauren could maybe do something to stop this?"

I don't know why Kristoff's mom thought, *Oh, Lauren bosses up to bullies*; perhaps she assumed that I was a popular kid. But when my mom told me what was up, I decided to try to do something.

I sent Jack a text message saying, "Hey, what are you up to?" knowing he would probably text back asking me the same. When he did, I lied, saying, "Oh I'm just with my good friend Kristoff right now."

"Kristoff? You hang out with that guy?"

"Oh yeah, we're really close. He's a family friend. We're just going to go grab lunch."

I was just letting Jack know that Kristoff's my boy, don't fuck with him anymore. After that, he was nice to Kristoff, and Kristoff's mom called my mom, crying, saying thank you. I felt pretty cool for a minute. Like a moral vigilante.

It was the same with my baby brother. If anyone fucked with Easton, I was bossing up. He's six foot two and as handsome as they come, but in high school he was tiny and had braces, and all he wanted to do was hang out with his little weird friends and play video games. People started messing with him, but when they found out he was my brother, they stopped. They were scared of me, because they knew I went insane when I saw other kids being bullied. I fought for my fellow weirdos because I had nothing to lose; those bullies weren't my friends. Plus, I knew what it felt like being bullied, and I hated that anyone had to feel like that, even for a second.

My mom started getting more phone calls from parents of kids in theater class, asking, "Can you have Lauren talk to so-and-so at school? They've really been tough on my son." I would say something, and they wouldn't get bullied anymore. It was pretty badass. Even though I was still being bullied myself at this time, their bullies were different from my bullies. My bullies were the mean-girl cheerleaders, their bullies were the jocks, and the jocks listened to me when I told them to leave my theater kids alone, because they thought I was hot. The way it all works is so stupid.

I've always had a mama bear in me, because my own mom had always taught me to put myself in other peoples' shoes, and when I did, it made me so mad, knowing that they were being picked on and made to feel sad and worthless every day. To this day, whenever I see someone being attacked, it makes me feel like I have to step up to the plate because not everyone is as tough as I am. I know what it feels like to be an outcast, but somehow, it upsets me more when I see it happen to other people. I have a visceral reaction when I come across people making fun of someone else, whether it's on TV or an innocent comment by people walking along the street. God forbid I ever hear people make fun of someone's bad skin—I see red when I hear anyone call another person "crater face," because I have been on the receiving end of comments like that.

Here's the thing, though . . . bullies often don't know that they're bullying you. And sometimes the people who are bullied turn into bullies. I have watched myself on TV and observed my reactions when I think someone is coming for me, or edging into my territory, and I've been shocked. My reactions have been completely over-the-top, sometimes. It's only since quitting alcohol that I've been able to have enough clarity and honesty with myself to be able to admit that sometimes, I become the very thing I claim to be fighting against. Good and bad live inside us all, and often, it's a daily battle to make sure the good side stays on top.

Skyline was definitely infested with toxic people, but compared to places like Brighton High School, Skyline was a sandbox. I remember going to Brighton's prom when I was sixteen, with a dude named Murphy, a senior there. He was super cute, Puerto Rican, and had a smile that could make a girl faint. We double-dated with Murphy's friend, who brought a girl named Roxanne as his date. Roxanne was also a sophomore and was drop-dead gorgeous, like a cross between Adriana Lima and Alessandra Ambrosio. I always told her that's who she reminded me of; she had a face that took your breath away, and, more important, she was sweet. As we finished up our predance dinner, Roxanne and I headed to the ladies' room to freshen up. As we walked back to our table, there they were—the Brighton Bitches. Looking back on them now, I have no idea why I was so intimidated by them. As we made our way past their table, they started taunting us.

"Whore," one of them said to me loudly.

Whore? I'd never even seen a dick in real life.

With high school being a war zone, I was grateful for the friendships I had had since birth, like Madison and Olivia. A little history on our trio: Madison's mom is Jami. Olivia's mom is Cid. My mom is Lisa. Cid, Jami, and Lisa had been their own little trio since junior high, and they are still a trio to this day. Jami and Cid both had three kids and were planning on having their final babies.

My mom, as you all know, was in no rush to do anything in life. I mean, she dated my dad for nearly eight years before even tying the knot. Jami and Cid sat my mom down and said, "If you want to have a baby with us you better get on board."

My mom decided to climb on board the baby train. Cid got pregnant with Olivia, then Jami got pregnant with Madison, then my mom got pregnant with me. The three of us would be ride-or-dies forever. Olivia and Madison would know the reason for every outburst I'd have, every horrible breakup, every scared moment; they'd be there. They were there when my dad had health scares; they'd witness my anxiety peak to unknown levels. They knew every scar and every wound, and I knew theirs.

Olivia was always the more traditional one of the three of us, while Madison and I were the ones with a screw loose, who chose entertainment as our future plans. Most of the other kids I knew in Utah had no specific ambitions. You just finish high school, then you go to the University of Utah, then you wait for your Mormon missionary boyfriend to return at the age of twenty-two, then you get married and make a lot of babies. No one had a master plan or a big dream, like Madi and me. We both wanted to be stars of showbiz, someway, somehow.

When Madison got her license, she would pick me up in her white Jetta with the tan interior and we would blast "Gangsta's Paradise" by Coolio, and head to our acting class. But no Hollywood story goes off without a hitch, and Madison and I had many ups and downs along the way, starting with when we were first "discovered" at Fashion Place mall in Salt Lake, by a man named Henry Lipton, owner of a modeling agency. He would often send scouts out to malls or restaurants around town, and if they saw a girl who had an interesting look, they would approach her and try to sign her. We couldn't believe when it happened to us while we were wandering around the mall. Like, that shit doesn't happen; someone doesn't just walk up to you, tell you that you're beautiful and they want to represent you. Henry gave us both his card and said we should call to set up a photo shoot to get comp cards. Our moms checked it out, and he was legit. I was thirteen and Madi was fourteen years old.

After our first encounter, our moms chatted with Henry often, and he advised us it was time to take photos for our books and our comp cards. A book is full of pictures of yourself showing diverse looks so potential clients can see your work. A comp card is something you leave with the client that has a picture of you on both front and back, your representation's name and contact, and all the stats.

Henry set up a shoot for us in San Diego, where we each had to pay $2,000 for our photographs. FACT: if you are interested in modeling, *never* pay that kind of money for pictures. We paid the two g's and headed to San Diego via a road trip. When we pulled up to the hotel where the shoot was taking place, we noticed a guy standing on the corner of the street, picking his nose. My mom laughed and said, "Oh, look, that's probably your photographer." And we all laughed.

After we parked and got into the hotel room, that same guy was, in fact, waiting for us, holding a camera. The photos we took were posted on the agency's website. I was in a bikini in one of them, and all the boys in the seventh grade would look at it during computer class until the school had to block the website.

At the time, I looked very awkward. I hadn't grown into my ears, I was covered in freckles, I was super thin and as tall back then as I am now, around five foot six. I thought I looked like an alien. Nonetheless, I started booking local modeling work, which eventually led to interest from bigger modeling agencies.

One day, an agent from Ford modeling agency in New York flew to Utah just to meet me. We met her at a hotel downtown, and she told my mom, "We'd love to move Lauren out to New York, have her start doing runway shows and really prep her to be a part of the industry." Because I was so tall for my age, they assumed I was going to be a six foot two Amazon woman by the time I was eighteen.

But my mom was very leery of it all. "I'm not sending my kid to New York City and getting her an apartment! She's thirteen!"

After the meeting, my mom said to me, "Look, if you really want to do this, we can make it happen, but you're going to miss out on a lot of what's fun about being a teenager." And I just knew, in the pit of my stomach, that she was right. I wasn't ready to be in that world. I wasn't a confident child. I didn't like the way I looked, and I was intimidated by everybody. I felt safe in Utah, with my family, and even though I was always being bullied, I did have friends who loved me and a family that made life magical. I didn't want to leave all that behind.

My mom wasn't a stage mom, but she did play a role in coming up with my first stage name. Lauren Burningham looked fucked-up on a headshot—too complicated—and people were always calling me "Loren Birmingham," which drove me nuts. I was a daddy's girl, so I didn't want to disrespect him by axing the family name; so I took his first name, Kent, as my last, and turned the *e* in Lauren to a *y*. Lauryn Kent. With my new headshots complete, and my new stage name, I was ready to go.

I hustled my way into as many gigs as I could. By fourteen, I wanted to take my craft more seriously, be more professional. The kids at school had no idea I was trying to act; I kept that to myself, just between Madi and me and a few friends I could trust. I never told anyone about my dream because I didn't want anyone to look at me with pity, or laugh at me, in case it never happened. But every audition we heard about, Madison and I would go together and hope at least one of us would book a job. She was my road dawg—"From the womb to the tomb."

Madison was a late bloomer, flat-chested for most of her life. (Fun fact: she lost her virginity at twenty-two, to a very well-known celebrity who I will not name.) Like me, she was bullied most of her school days, and it made me so upset. She was the sweetest little human being ever, and a very, very beautiful girl. She wasn't a flirt, but I think because she was so pretty, it made the other girls resent her.

She would call me crying, saying, "What is happening? They're making fun of me because I'm flat-chested."

I'd say, "Well, I've known you since you were a little baby, and I don't care when you grow boobs, if ever."

Then my mom would call Madi's mom, Jami, and say, "Do you want to take Madison out of school and we can all go to LA together?" Many times, Madison and I escaped to LA together with our moms, to get away from the shit we were dealing with at school. And together, looking at the Hollywood sign in the distance, we would wonder, *How long will it be before our dreams came true here, some way, somehow?*

My mom and I were on vacation in Santa Monica with Kristin (the woman who made me sign my fame contract) and her daughter, Candice. We had eaten lunch at the Ivy, a fancy restaurant on Robertson Boulevard, and were waiting for our car when a Porsche Cayenne zoomed past. The driver (let's call him Rick because it rhymes with prick) was looking at us. He quickly made a U-turn, pulled up, and got out.

"Hi," he said, looking at me. "I drove past and saw you and had to turn around."

Then he looked at my mom.

"Hi, I'm Rick," he said, holding his hand out. He said he was an agent at one of the top three agencies in LA.

We chatted for a while, and I told him I was an actress and what I wanted to do with my career. We set a meeting. Afterward, we looked him up—he had been written about in the *Hollywood Reporter*, labeled as one of the top one hundred people to know in Hollywood. Clearly, he was a Somebody. This was exciting!

My mom and I went to his fancy offices and we had our first meeting with Rick, getting into more detail about what interested me, what shows I liked, what coaching I'd had. He gave me pages for a cold read (when you are given a scene on the spot to act out) and it went great. He set me up with an audition for *The OC* playing Mischa Barton's younger sister. (Spoiler alert: I didn't get it . . . not even a callback.) Then Rick told me he wanted to take me to meet some casting directors around town. My mom and Candice's mom had to leave for Utah the following day, so Candice and I stayed on at Candice's aunt's house in LA, and she agreed to take me to the meetings and pick me up afterward.

The morning Rick was supposed to take me to meet casting directors, I felt like my life was about to change. My stomach was churning, and it was hard to breathe as I got dressed that morning. I didn't know yet that this was my intuition warning me.

We pulled up to the agency; I jumped out of the car and got in the elevator. I entered the grand lobby I had been to once before, where Rick was waiting for me, and followed him to his office. He seemed different now we were alone. Not so warm.

"What's wrong with you?" he said, looking at my face.

"What do you mean?"

"You look terrible. I can't take you anywhere looking like that. These casting directors will think I'm insane for even bringing you in."

I was too stunned to say anything for a moment. Then, quietly, I told him I felt sick. I needed to use the restroom and call my friend's aunt to come and get me.

"Good, you do that," he said.

In the bathroom, I looked at myself in the mirror, and my eyes were glazed, my face pale. I called Candice; they weren't far away, and she said she would flip around and come get me. I went back to Rick's office, feeling ashamed. He led me to the elevator, but a different one this time. It looked like a service elevator.

We got in, and halfway down, he stopped the elevator. He came toward me, put his right hand on the elevator wall, arm extended, and leaned in to kiss me. I turned my face and put my hand up.

"I'm fourteen," I said to Rick, twenty-eight-year-old "agent to the stars."

He backed off and looked at me with disgust.

"I think we're on the wrong elevator," he said, and acted like nothing had happened.

When I got in the car, I told Candice and her aunt what happened, and immediately called my mom, sobbing. My mom beat herself up over this for a long while and said she felt like she had failed at protecting me. I didn't feel that way at all. We were kind, moral people from Utah. We were naive to Hollywood. We were naive to the Ricks of the world.

My mom decided to call the agency and speak to him about what had happened. When she called, there was a pause on the line.

"Rick is no longer with our agency," the receptionist said, and hung up.

I don't know if there were cameras in that service elevator, or if something else had happened, but somehow, that slimeball resigned or got fired at some point in between him trying to kiss me in the elevator and my mom's phone call. He was a man in a position of power, hitting on a fourteen-year-old girl because he knew she had a dream and would probably stay silent. I don't know what happened to him, but I hope he never was allowed to work around teenage girls again.

I've never shared this story before. I never felt like I needed to, because I wasn't traumatized by it long term. Mainly disgusted. It was just a story in my life, that I, like my mom, learned something from. Not all people are good and worthy of your trust, and bullies come in all shapes and sizes. From the Brighton Bitches to the bigshot Hollywood agent who preys on girls in service elevators—

when you have a dream, there's always someone who wants to tear it down. So you better be ready.

—————

Madi and I had a plan to move out to LA together once we'd finished high school. But Madi had started making mad moves, got a manager, and ended up ditching high school and moving to LA when she was sixteen. When she was eighteen she became the hottest reason to see the new Adam Sandler movie *Grown Ups*. You go, girl.

As for me, I ping-ponged back and forth about whether I should move to LA or stay put and finish school. Madison had put the pedal to the metal and made the move, and I admired her ability to grind. She just made things happen. But I was heartbroken when she left, and it was really hard to keep the dream alive without her.

On a trip out to visit Madi in her new home in LA, she offered to take me to her manager's office and see if he'd sign me, too. His name was Petras and his office was in the building of a major studio network, which intimidated my socks off; but I pulled it together. We headed up to the twenty-second floor, where he let me share my hopes and dreams and aspirations. I waited for him to respond, hopeful.

"You have a very thick Utah accent," he told me. "And you wear too much makeup."

Bitch, I was breaking out, so I was covering that shit up. But I stayed quiet and listened to what he had to say.

Petras said if I wanted to be taken seriously, I needed to "go back to Utah and work very hard." And that was it. He could have said it nicer or softer, but he didn't.

I exited his office feeling defeated, and yes, I did cry. When you're a teenager and someone tells you that you and your accent suck, it's crushing. Enough to make you think, *Maybe I should just give up. Maybe this is never going to happen for me.* Or even worse, *Maybe he's right.*

My mom held my face in her hands and gave me words I still live by today: "Lauren, you're holding on to all the negatives. He also gave you advice. You need to work, get better at your craft. Hold on to that and throw out the negatives. It's not worth anything; it's Monopoly money. So you're allowed to be upset about it for the next ten minutes, then you have to put it in the trash."

I walked out of that room, and I held on to those ten minutes tight, so I could obsess over every little detail. Then I let it go. And I focused on the lesson.

That's how I try to look at life now. It's a bank account. People who have things to say that are valuable—put that in the bank. It can come in the form of you giving me a simple compliment or a hard piece of advice. The rest deserves no more than ten minutes of my life.

I went back to Utah, called my agency there, TMG, and asked for their list of recommended acting coaches in Utah. I enrolled in a three-day, twelve-hour intensive scene-study class. Every Monday and Wednesday night you'd find me at Rob Diamond's, my regular go-to acting class. And I hired a dialect coach for $100 an hour to fix my "Utah twang." I'll never let it go entirely, though. To this day, I get a lot of DMs and comments calling me "Lauren from Utah," as though it's an insult to me. Well, I am Lauren, and if you can pronounce it correctly you are more than welcome to call me that. And I am from Utah, in fact, I am a proud Utahn and will forever call it home. Utah is my heart. It's where I learned values and where my family taught me to have a high sense of self. High enough to shoot for the stars.

chapter five

THERE'S A FIRST TIME
FOR EVERYTHING

*W*HEN I WAS A teenager, one of my best friends was a girl named Dani Wolfe. The Wolfes are and always have been badass women. Dani was my sister heathen and played a huge role in my survival in grade school, and Dani's mom, Kelly, was effortlessly fabulous, always in designer wear, with her cute Chanel flats and dainty, expensive jewelry. I wanted to be her when I grew up.

Kelly was the GOAT; she bought Dani and me a golf cart, painted it hot pink, and laced it with subwoofers and chrome rims, so Dani and I could ride around the neighborhood. Everything was all-day fun at the Wolfe residence, which was decked to the nines and situated on a sprawling plot of land alongside several other multimillion-dollar mansions.

When Dani and I were fourteen, we would do things like "borrow" her dad's car and drive down the street to pick up Chinese food, then go back to her house and watch *Sex and the City*. One time, Dani and I caked on a few inches of makeup to go on a Vespa ride around the neighborhood. Soon enough, a cop car came up behind us, lights flashing, and pulled us over—apparently, driving a Vespa underage without a license is no laughing matter.

"Don't worry, our moms are cool, they'll have our backs," Dani whispered as the cops called our parents. I knew for sure our moms would have our backs, but I also knew my mom would be pissed that her fourteen-year-old was running around wearing more makeup than a drag queen at Pride. And when my mom showed up, to the cops' annoyance, instead of scolding me for breaking the law, the first thing she did was rub my cheeks and say, "Honey, you're wearing too much makeup."

That winter, Kelly took Dani and me on a girls' trip to Aspen. Everything was within walking distance of the hotel; the ski hill was right there, little shops were everywhere, and it was very bougie fabulous. Dani and I were out roaming the village one day when we walked past a sign that read PSYCHIC.

"Should we go in?" Dani asked.

"All right," I said. "That sounds fun."

We sat down in front of the psychic, an older woman from

India. I remember her words exactly—she looked at me and said, "How long have you had a boyfriend with big hair?"

I was shook. My puppy-love boyfriend at the time was Matt, who had amazing hair and wore a pick in it every day to school. He was so dreamy, and we'd hold hands and peck each other on the cheek.

"I see you will be with a much older man," the psychic continued. "I see you are both in entertainment. You live in California in hills. You will have one child. I see two other children, but they don't come from your womb. You may adopt, or something, but they don't come from you."

I did *not* believe this shit. Everyone know that I was going to marry an athlete, become a WAG, have six kids, and one day win an Oscar. We walked out of there thinking she was just a fake, even though she had, somehow, figured out that my boyfriend had big hair. If you'd asked me then if this was to be my destiny, I would have laughed. I knew exactly what grown-up life would look like for me, and it wasn't that. As I often say, us Virgos always have everything mapped out. . . .

By the time I started high school, I was still very inexperienced, a late bloomer, when it came to love and sex. Most of my friends were touching pee-pees in high school, but I didn't even make out with a boy until I was in ninth grade. I knew what sex was, of course—one of my friends' little brothers had shown us his parents' sex books when I was eight or nine. I told my mom, and she explained that sex is what adults do when they're in a relationship, and maybe I shouldn't be looking at that stuff quite yet.

Nothing was hidden from me, though, and sometimes I would see things on TV that I didn't quite understand. I'm not talking boobies, drugs, and orgies—we never had HBO—but I was never afraid to ask her what was going on when actors started getting into sex scenes. No question was too inappropriate, no subject was untouchable as far as my mom was concerned. She always made it clear that when I was old enough, I would be able to make my own mind up about sex and what I wanted to do with it. To this day, I feel like that was a healthy approach for her to have taken as a parent because when you make kids fear things, it warps their relationship with it. They become curious or obsessed. But I never felt like there was anything wrong or inappropriate about sex. I just knew that when I was old enough, if I wanted to touch a weiner, I could go right ahead. I definitely was in no rush. And neither was my first real boyfriend, Eddie, a very short Tongan boy who I started dating in ninth grade.

Eddie was a sophomore in high school and the star running back on Skyline's football team. He was perfect, except his family members were all super-strict Mormons, and they had banned Eddie from having a girlfriend, which made things hard for us romantically. We could never be seen together at football games, for instance; I would have to sit with my mom and try very hard to make it look like we weren't a couple.

Eddie didn't do drugs or drink, which was fine by me, because I didn't do those things, either. But his family was a real drag. They didn't let him go out, and for the year and a half I was with him, I had to go to dances by myself because Eddie's mom made him take his sister to every single school dance.

Looking back, it was kind of a waste of my time. He was a real Goody Two-shoes, too scared to touch my boobs, and he definitely didn't want me touching his weiner. Physically, emotionally, and spiritually, there was nowhere for this relationship to go. We were fundamentally incompatible and soon found ourselves at a dead end.

Despite my frustration, I stayed loyal to him, believing that love conquers all. In my head, all the pain of abstinence and lying was worth it because I was going to marry this guy one day. When I told my dad, he laughed his ass off.

"Lauren, you're sixteen, I have a feeling you're probably not going to marry this kid."

"You're wrong!" I said. "He's going to the NFL, then we're getting married and having six babies. Two girls, four boys."

Eventually, my patience ran out. His religion was too much of a lifestyle. So one day, standing in our front yard on the cordless, I called and told him, "I can't be with you anymore, Eddie." I was crying. "You need to be with someone who's Mormon."

Afterward, I lay in bed listening to "Anytime" by Brian McKnight on replay.

I can't remember why we fell apart
From something that was so meant to be, yeah

But Eddie had to go. I couldn't be with someone who wanted to hide his relationship with me.

Enter Johnny, a six-foot-four Samoan with tribal tattoos and baby-making bedroom eyes. His dad looked like the Rock, therefore Johnny looked like the offspring of the Rock—a dream to look at. All the girls went crazy for him. Luckily, there were two of them to choose from, as Johnny had a twin brother, Rocco. And yes, Rocco was equally as tall and bangin'.

Johnny and I started dating my junior year, thanks to my friend Liv, daughter of my mom's friend Cid. Liv and Johnny were both seniors and went to Cottonwood High together. Madison had already dipped to LA, and school was getting rough for me, so Liv and I started spending a lot of time together. She was a cheerleader (one of the very few I liked) and was always known as a popular girl, but things shifted in her senior year when her fellow pom-pom-shaking dipshit friends turned on her. As y'all know, I bully the bullies for the people I care for, so I would show up to basketball and football games where she was cheering and defend my friend if needed. It helped when Johnny was there, playing. Flirting with him helped take my mind off my breakup with PG Eddie, my Mormon virgin prince, who was still mad at me for dumping him.

Liv and I had a deal worked out—for the dances at my high school, I would get one of my male friends to invite Liv to be his date, and she would do the same for me for dances at her school. That way, we'd always have a girl ally by our side at the dances. When the winter formal rolled around, Liv said she was going to tell Johnny to ask me to be his date. Johnny picked me up and, y'all, he looked too good. My mom took our picture and we headed off to the festivities. He was being sweet to me, but at some point in the night, I don't know why, I got really bratty with him. After the dance, Liv and I ditched our dates and headed to Liv's house. He continued to text and call me, acting sweet, and I continued to be a dick.

Later in the week I found out that after Liv and I went home, Johnny slept with a girl. When I heard the news, I felt sick to my stomach. I knew I'd been a bitch to him and he wasn't my boyfriend and was therefore allowed to do whatever he wanted—but *sex*? Having sex was a foreign concept to me, and I kept picturing them together, obsessing over every detail. I was furious and, maybe, after eighteen months of Bible Boy, a little turned on . . . but mainly furious.

Johnny tried to explain, saying he'd wanted to be with me that night but I was being mean to him. It didn't matter how much he apologized, I was grossed out, and my soul was crushed, so I took my T-Mobile Sidekick and blocked him. He started using Rocco's phone to blow me up, instead. When I heard Johnny's voice on the end of the line, I yelled, "This is your bad!"

"I know!" he said.

"Listen, Johnny, I don't know why you're still calling me, because I'm not that type of girl."

"Lauren, I was upset that you ditched me," he explained. "Give me a second chance. I'll make it up to you."

Maybe it wasn't the most romantic start, but I liked that Johnny could stand up to me. That he could be straightforward about how he felt.

I don't remember when I got over Johnny banging it out with another girl, but finally, I let my guard down and allowed him to take me on a real date. When we kissed, I realized this was what I'd wanted all along—a guy who was confident, sexual, and unafraid. Hallelujah.

When I first got with Johnny, he was a little rough around the edges. He had some questionable friends—one night, boys' night turned sour because one of his buddies kept calling me bitch, and Johnny took him outside for a beating. I wasn't there, but I heard all about it. I thought it was cute and romantic that he'd defended my honor like that, except the next night, the guy came back with his homies and their guns and shot at Johnny's house. Luckily everyone was safe, but when my dad found out, he said he didn't want me going over there for a while.

Johnny was on the verge of not graduating and had community service to complete for some trouble he had gotten into, so every day after school, I would drive to his house, help him get all of his homework done—and all of his extra credit—to get his grades up. I found places for us to volunteer on the weekends so he could complete his community service. I got him back on track and helped him get a job so he could afford a car. It was fun, being the woman behind the man.

I was so proud to attend his graduation with his family . . . so proud when he got his community service done and bought a car. He even pulled money together to buy me gifts throughout our relationship and sent me beautiful handwritten love letters. We spent every single day together. We were young, but Johnny was someone I saw myself spending the rest of my life with.

For the first few months we were together, I let him finger bang me, but nothing more. We would have sleepovers, which our parents seemed cool with, but behind closed doors, my dad was a little worried. My mom told him, "Kent, she doesn't have friends in school. He makes her happy. If they want to have sex, they are gonna have it whether it's here or somewhere else. Let it go."

It just sort of happened, one afternoon after school. We went into his bedroom, where he had red light bulbs in all the light fixtures, so it looked like a photo darkroom. He put on some music, and we laid on his bed and started to fool around. We both knew it was going to happen, so he pulled out a condom—also red. He slid it on like a pro, which he was, and before I knew it, it was happening. "Lollipop" by Lil Wayne was playing at the exact moment I lost my virginity.

Shawty wanna thug, bottles in the club
Shawty wanna hump, you know I'd like to touch ya lovely
    lady lumps

It was apropos AF, but afterward, I felt like my innocence was gone, like I wasn't a child anymore, and that made me sad. My head was starting to spin, so I told Johnny I was going home and I'd be back later.

When I went back to his house that evening, he had some friends over and they were drinking in the basement, blasting music. Normally I would have headed down to kick it with them. Instead, I grabbed a blanket and pillows off the couch and laid on the floor of his parents' family room. I texted Johnny to let him know I was there, and he came upstairs and asked me if I was okay. Cuddled up like a little snug bug, I said yes. He made his way over to me, got underneath the blanket, and we watched *Ratatouille* together while his friends continued to party. In his arms, I felt safe again and I realized I was glad to have lost my virginity to this gorgeous soul. After that, sex was no problem for me at all. We were like jackrabbits. I wanted to hump all the time—there was just one small issue. Blow jobs.

I told my friend Sophia, and she told me not to worry so much. But I was worried about biting off my boyfriend's wiener.

"Lauren, you should at least *try*. That's a guy's most favorite thing ever." Sophia was a slutty theater geek with huge double-D boobs, and the boys went crazy over her. She and her older sister, Monica, were both stunning Italian girls with dark hair and giant lips, and were super confident sexually. I knew she knew how to give a great BJ. So to help me solve my predicament, they took me to the supermarket for a little training simulation.

Sophia and Monica searched in the dessert section for the perfect Popsicle, one that was of adequate size—a Minute Maid lemonade push pop. We got one each, and then, in the parking lot, they showed me exactly how to do it. I remember thinking that this was the kind of sex ed I wished they'd teach in schools.

Afterward, I went over to Johnny's house and gave him my very first blow job, like a champion. He didn't know it was coming, and his mind was blown. At the end, though, I sat there, mouth full, waiting for instructions. Sophia and Monica had forgotten to tell me the aftercare protocol.

"Do I swallow it?" I managed to ask him.

"Yeah! You should swallow it!" he said.

I gulped and looked at him. I was now officially a swallower. I mean, this boy was over the moon, I'm telling you.

We were pretty responsible, as far as sexually active teenagers go. Sophia and I would make trips to Planned Parenthood, more often than I'd like to admit—we called it P-squared.

"Hey, want to run to P-squared today?"

"Yes, I need to stock up on condoms."

And when we weren't so responsible, or if a condom would break, we'd hit P-squared for some Plan B.

Everything was good, and I was so in love with Johnny that everything else seemed to fade into insignificance, including my dreams. Love seemed so much deeper than ambition, now that I'd had a taste of it (in all ways). Why would I follow in Madison's footsteps and move to LA, when I had this hunk of love here with me in Utah?

But once I graduated from high school, it was time to start making some real choices. I tried to think of ways I could make good money while still being a presence on TV and stay in Utah. I went on auditions for news channel spots where they'd hire a girl to come out and talk about a new car for a pretty decent annual salary. That seemed like the best option for me. *If I could only land that kind of job, I could just stay in Utah, Johnny and I will get married, and we'll have six babies.* I was so happy in my little world with Johnny, the bigger picture of what I wanted became invisible. But deep inside, I grappled with the sense that I would have to put my deepest hopes on the back burner in order to settle down. That's what happens to a lot of girls in Utah . . . maybe girls everywhere. You find your person and *they* become your dream.

At seventeen, I had yet to have a drink. Not one drop of alcohol had ever crossed my lips. I just never had the urge, not even when everyone was getting wasted around me. But when I got to my senior year, I realized there was a strong chance I might graduate high school without ever having known what it felt like to be drunk. I started to panic. The FOMO was intense, and as usual, I began overthinking. What if I was missing out on one of the most important milestones of being a teenager? What if my sobriety was about to ruin my life? I had to fix this situation.

I texted Sophia saying I wanted to get drunk for the first time, but I wanted to do it at her house, supervised (strong Virgo moves).

"All right, this weekend we'll get you drunk for the first time; we'll take care of you," she said.

Her parents had bought her and her sister a house in Foothill, and they threw parties there every weekend, so I went with Johnny to her house party, and got shit-faced on Smirnoff vodka and Coca-Cola. (Flat Coke, by the way.) You know when you watch *Clueless* as a kid and you think, *Oh, so that's what high school's like?* This was me living my *Clueless* moment, finally living the high school life I'd seen in the movies.

The feeling was liberating, somehow. Anxiety had always been a normal part of my daily existence, but being drunk, I couldn't even remember what I was anxious about. For the first time in my life, all my stress and inhibitions seemed to just . . . float away. I wasn't ashamed. I wasn't worrying what people thought of me. I was just relaxed and having fun.

I remember lying on the couch, spinning.

Johnny asked me, "Are you okay?"

"Yes," I said, smiling, not giving a shit about anything.

Being drunk reminded me of that feeling I had in theater class, where I could detach from myself and pretend to be someone else. On that couch, I remember thinking, *So this is how you stop feeling bad stuff. This is how you get to be someone who doesn't care about anything.*

After nearly three years together, Johnny sat me down and hit me with some surprising news—he'd enrolled in a community college, Cerritos College, on a football scholarship, and was moving to LA. Norwalk, to be precise, a south LA suburb. When he told me, I had mixed emotions. On the one hand, I was happy for him, on the other, I couldn't help but feel betrayed. I was nineteen going on twenty years old and had assumed we were going to start building a life together, close to our families in Salt Lake. I pushed those thoughts out of my head once I realized that, actually, this could be great—if he moved to LA, then I could go with him! We would embark on a new life and live out our big dreams together!

I wished we could have rented an apartment together, but he needed to be close to school and I needed to be close to LA for acting, so he moved into his aunt's house in Long Beach, about forty minutes out of LA, and I moved in with Madison and Danielle at their apartment in Studio City, sharing a room with Madison. Until then, I had always called myself Lauren, but Danielle introduced me to everyone in LA with my childhood nickname, Lala. From then on, Lala was my name whether I liked it or not.

I found a fit modeling company (the same one I would eventually sign up with again when I moved back to LA four years later), and that became my job. But things didn't go as I'd hoped. I didn't go on any auditions at all. I was a little lost. I had followed my boyfriend to the big city and assumed everything would work itself out. The universe, of course, had other plans.

One weekend, Johnny was over at our apartment, and one of Danielle's friends showed up with her little sister. She was cool and beautiful, and I really liked her. The next time I saw her, she took me aside. Apparently, I wasn't the only one she'd made a dazzling impression on.

"Hey, I wanted to let you know that Johnny tried reaching out to me."

"What do you mean?"

"Yeah, he hit me up on AOL Instant Messenger. He wasn't inappropriate or anything, but I just thought it was very weird."

My mind was racing. Why the fuck would he ever need to get ahold of this girl? He didn't know her from Adam, he had only met her one time. At *my* apartment. I felt that feeling in my gut, the intuition. It was trying to tell me something. Johnny had slowly been detaching from me, for a long time. And if he was willing to hit on a girl from my own circle of friends, I could only imagine how many other girls he was reaching out to. No matter which way I thought about it, I knew it was wrong. My dad would never have pulled anything so sleazy when he was dating my mom. I felt utterly disrespected and knew instantly that this wasn't the man I was going to marry. We were done.

I broke up with him over text and didn't even give him the chance to explain himself. He tried to apologize and came to my apartment complex several times, trying to talk to me, but this time, I wasn't giving out any second chances. I told the security guard to never let him up. When I lose trust in someone, it's very hard for me to want to stay around them. Johnny ended up moving home a few months later and we never spoke again.

After our breakup, I fell into a depression. I drank bottles of red wine every night. It felt like I was doing nothing with my life. Living in LA was nothing like what I'd dreamed it would be. In fact, it was amplifying all my deepest insecurities. I'd drive to my fit-modeling jobs, feeling like people were looking at my car, judging it, looking at me with expressions that said, *She's not that pretty. She's not good enough for this town.* I already lacked self-esteem, and being in LA was just amplifying every feeling of self-doubt I had. Six months after moving, I called my mom and said, "I need you to come get me. I can't do this anymore."

January 2010, I moved home, thinking I would go to college and live a normal life in Salt Lake, close to my family. But weeks after moving back to Utah, Carter, an up-and-coming football star, wrote me on Facebook messenger. I had been casually talking to one of his teammates, and Carter must have seen me on that guy's Facebook page. He told me I was special and beautiful, and asked me to come and see him. Those words were what got me on a plane back to LA, where, just like the psychic in Aspen had predicted, I would soon find myself living a life I never could have imagined. . . .

chapter six

MY BODY, MY CHOICE

*B*Y 2013, CARTER AND I had been seeing each other long-distance for more than a year, me living in Utah, modeling and trying to figure out what the hell I was doing with my life, and him kicking ass playing college football. I looked up to him like some sort of god, and when you put someone on a pedestal like that, it's easy for them to lose respect. After a while, Carter's behavior indicated to me that I wasn't good enough, that I was lucky to be with him. And that meant that when we were together, I often felt self-conscious, ugly, full of self-doubt. When we weren't together, he would take days to respond to texts and rarely took my calls. I wish I could talk to my younger self and tell her "You are amazing. You are beautiful. Don't kiss his ass." Hindsight is 20/20.

It didn't help that my skin had started breaking out, further diminishing my confidence. When everyone else was fighting cystic acne together in junior high and in high school, my skin was fabulous, with rarely even a blemish. But things changed as I got older. I tried every medicated face wash, organic makeup, vitamin and pill to cure my acne. I changed my diet, cut out alcohol, but nothing seemed to work. I never felt secure enough to show Carter my skin, so when I would go to LA to visit him, I would always pack a nighttime makeup bag filled with bareMinerals makeup that I would put on before bed. I'd cover up the little blemishes, and make it look subtle, but enough that Carter wouldn't think, *Shit, she is broken the fuck out.*

When I think about this time in my life I feel sad. How could I feel so ashamed of something so surface level? When I would get upset about my skin, my mom would say, "Lauren, remember it is just skin. There are people who have lost their limbs. Bumps on your face, not a big deal. It's not forever. We will get it taken care of." She was absolutely right, and I wished I could adopt my mom's outlook on life, but I wasn't built like her. My mind didn't work the same way. Instead, my thoughts spiraled deeper and deeper into self-loathing, and obsession with this man who gave me just enough to keep me hanging, but never enough to make me happy.

A blizzard hit Salt Lake City one weekend, the same weekend Carter flew up to visit me. He was only staying four days, and it was the first time he'd ever visited Utah. I was so excited for him to come to my house, see where I grew up, and meet my beautiful family. Anything to help me feel closer to this man I loved so much.

It had been at least a month since we'd last seen each other, so once we were alone together in my bedroom, it was on. Usually we were careful in bed and practiced safe sex, but one night, both of us got a little drunk and were ready to go, with or without a condom. The sex was a little rough, from behind, and we wound up practicing the pullout method that night. These days, when anyone says to me "We pull out," I'm like, "Oh God. You're playing with fire." Because that method does not always work.

We'd already had a few conversations about what would happen if I got pregnant. My parents never condoned having a baby out of wedlock, but it was by no means frowned upon. My parents raised us to be free thinkers and make our own decisions, and it wasn't taboo to move in with your lover or have a baby with them before you were married. But Carter's family had different views on things, and he had told me that his mom would be very upset if he were ever to get someone pregnant out of wedlock. He came from a very Christian background, and when his mom and I would drive to games together, she'd always have gospel music or pastor radio playing. She was a very traditional, by the book, God-fearing lady in that way, so I always respected that and knew that Carter and I could never get pregnant unless we were married first. With this in mind, not long after Carter's visit, I took a pregnancy test just to be safe. To my relief, it came out negative.

Super Bowl Sunday rolled around a few weeks after Carter's visit to Utah. The 49ers were playing the Baltimore Ravens, the team I grew up watching (there are no pro teams in Utah, so that's just the team my family and I watched). I had my Ravens shirt on, as did my mom and my dad, and when Beyoncé performed at half-time, I changed into a Beyoncé tank top.

The Ravens won. I got obliterated.

It was the best day ever.

The next day, however, was not.

I was very sick the next morning, sicker than a dog. It felt like I was having the world's longest, shittiest hangover, and it lasted all day. The next day, too. And it lingered.

A couple more weeks passed. I was working a nanny job at the time, which meant picking up a little girl from school and dropping her off at tumbling class. It was easy enough work, but one day, I had to have my mom cover for me, because I was feeling so sick and nauseous. The only thing that made the sickness lift a little was taking superhot baths, so hot I'd nearly pass out.

When I wasn't in the bath, I felt like I was going to vomit, and I couldn't stomach anything except watermelon and Diet Coke. The following day, I was still feeling nauseated, so my mom offered to take over driving the little girl to tumbling again, suggesting I come with her, just to get out of the house and get some fresh air. I said yes, and as we were pulling out of the driveway, I opened the passenger door and threw up.

"Mom, I think this is the worst hangover I've ever had," I said.

"How does it feel?" she asked me.

"I'm beyond nauseated," I said. "And it's really bad in the morning."

"Lauren, have you started your period?"

I thought about it and realized I hadn't. "Fuck."

As soon as we got home, I rushed upstairs and pulled out the pregnancy test pack I'd bought a few weeks back. There was a second test in there, so I peed on it and the result was immediate. Double lines. I was knocked up. I must have taken the first test too soon, before my body had started producing enough pregnancy hormones for the test to detect them.

I ran downstairs. My mom was on the phone with someone.

"Mom, it's positive." I started sobbing, feeling numb and helpless.

"Okay," my mom said. "We need to make an appointment at the doctor, just to make sure." I could see the worry in her face.

"No, we need to go now. Planned Parenthood is still open."

So there I was, in oversized sweatpants at four in the afternoon, with long, egg-shell blue Kylie Jenner nails, rolling up to Planned Parenthood with my mom to find out if I really was preggo. God bless Planned Parenthood. Not just because of my experience with them, but because it's a place so many girls could go and feel safe talking about the things they couldn't discuss at home. Even if you're broke as a joke, Planned Parenthood will take care of you, and I've always admired that.

"What would you do if you were me?" I asked my mom in the waiting room. My mom had always represented safety, and I turned to her whenever I wasn't sure about what the "right" thing to do was. I was always very by the book. I looked up to my parents and was not rebellious in any way because my family had always been so open with me. I remember the expression on her face so vividly. "If I were you, I would not have that baby," she said.

My mom would never have voiced her opinion to me if I hadn't asked for it. But I needed it more than anything at that moment in time. If I had said, "Mom, thank you for your advice, but I want to keep this baby," she would have been right by my side. No way would she ever leave me in the dust. My mom and dad would have stepped up to the plate, like champions, because they always supported every decision that I made, and with or without Carter, if I'd wanted to keep the baby, my mom and dad would have helped me raise that kid. But I'd asked for her opinion, and I got it. Her words were gold to me; she had never steered me wrong and always knew what was best for me. So when she told me she didn't think it was a good idea for me to have the baby, every cell in my body knew she was right. It was what my heart was telling me, anyway; she had just confirmed it.

They called my name, I went in the back, peed in a cup, and the results came—positive. They gauged me at about eight weeks along. When the nurse asked me what I wanted to do, I said, with pain in my voice, "I'm not going to have it."

"You're choosing abortion?"

I nodded my head. I couldn't even bring myself to say the word. I'd always felt weird saying it. Even more so now that I was about to have one myself.

Utah state law says that a woman seeking to have an abortion must attend at least one counseling session before the procedure, and then you're supposed to wait seventy-two hours before you can go through with it. I knew no matter what happened in the meeting, my mind was made up, and the choice I was making was the right one. For me, but also for Carter, who was far from ready to be a father. He still needed to graduate from college. He had come from a rough neighborhood and had managed to work his way out of it. He had a bright future ahead of him, and I didn't want this to derail him. For that reason, I decided not to mention it to Carter until after the mandatory abortion meeting, which happened to fall on February 14, Valentine's Day.

At the counselor's office, chairs were set up in a circle, about twenty of them. They had tried to make the place look homey, like a Mormon living room with little inspirational quotes on the wall and drapes on the window. Maybe I was the only pregnant person seeking an abortion in Salt Lake, because it was just me and the counselor in the room that day.

"Before I start, I want you to know that you are not a bad person," she said. "If you choose abortion, we're going to support you, and if you choose to have this baby, we're going to support you. There's no right or wrong decision here."

The second the words came out of her mouth, I broke down in tears. This was such an emotionally charged choice for me, and to feel accepted and supported by this kind stranger, no matter what I chose, sent waves of relief through my body. She hugged me and showed me some books.

"Right now, your paperwork says you're about eight weeks. So your baby is about the size of a raspberry." She showed me pictures, and everything she said seemed very fact-based. No judgment in her voice, nor persuasion.

"If you decide to choose abortion, there are two options, Lauren. You can take a pill in the comfort of your own home, or you can choose to do it in the clinic. If you decide to have the baby, here's when you'll likely give birth, and these are some of the vitamins you'll need to take." She told me October 4 was my projected due date.

I left the meeting feeling overly stimulated. I needed to tell Carter now. I needed him to be my partner through this, and give me comfort, give me love. I hated that I'd been so careless while he was in town, but he had played his part, too, and we should deal with the repercussions together. I called Carter, over and over, but he never picked up. This wasn't unusual. My heart was breaking, like it had so many times before.

When I got home, my sweet family was hanging out, heating up leftovers from the night before, watching TV. They'd all had such a normal day while I'd been making the biggest decision of my life. The only person who knew was my mom.

My dad, sweet caretaker as always, asked me if I was feeling better.

"Kind of," I said. I took a blanket and laid down on the heater vent on the floor; my go-to spot. My dad came over and gave me a plate of Indian food. Normally I'd go ham on a plate like this, but that night, it made me want to hurl. I didn't tell my dad that, though. I just looked at my mom, who was sitting on the couch, and said in a low tone, "Nothing like a plate of saag paneer to soothe my womb." We both chuckled a bit. It felt good to cut the serious shit, just for a moment.

Later that night, I sat on the edge of my bed, fixating on whether I would hear from Carter anytime soon. My dad walked in, looking sad.

"Sweetie, Grandma passed away," he said, fighting back tears. His mom, my sweet Mormon grandma, Mary-Lynn, had lost her fight with cancer. I couldn't believe this was all happening at the same time. I stood up and I hugged my dad, tears rolling down both of our faces, and at that precise moment, Carter finally decided to get back to me. Via text.

How was your day?

I was drained. In a fog. How could I possibly explain everything over text? So I responded the only way I felt I could.

My day was okay. My grandma died.

I refused to tell him I was pregnant over text. He sent me condolences, and I wished he would pick up the phone to call me so I could talk to him, share with him the full extent of what was going on, but he didn't. So I left it there. I didn't have the emotional strength to call him again, only for him to ignore my call. As much as I wished Carter could be there for me, I realized I was going to have to go through this without him.

The day of my abortion, my mom took me to the clinic. Inside, an old TV in the corner played *Jerry Springer,* and the place had a tired, government-owned ambiance, kind of like the DMV. One girl in there, clearly still in high school, sobbed on her boyfriend's shoulder. Some of the women in there clearly did not want to do this, and one of them ended up leaving. Another girl stood with her boyfriend at the cashier's window, desperately trying to figure out how they were going to pay for this, trying to get on a payment plan because she was days away from hitting the latest point in a pregnancy where you can legally have an abortion. It was all so sad.

I was called into a room where the procedure would be carried out, and the nurses asked me to lie on the gurney. They used an ultrasound machine and told me I was at nine weeks. Then they started the abortion, with a vacuum that they put up your vagina to basically suck the fetus out of you. I wasn't expecting it to be so painful, like the most excruciating cramps I have ever experienced in my life. Friends who'd had abortions before told me they'd been sedated and didn't feel anything, but I'd had no sedation or anesthesia, and was fully aware of what was happening. Tears streamed down my face from the pain.

One of the nurses, seeing my distress, came over and held my hand. She looked into my eyes, and I looked into hers as the whole thing happened. I happened to be wearing a little bracelet that my mom had brought me from Belize, with a little painting of Jesus on it. Even though I don't practice any religion, I do believe that Jesus is the son of God, and I believe in God as my higher power. I remember the nurse started playing with my bracelet, and told me that it was very beautiful. It was her attempt at distracting me, and I was grateful for it. She was the angel I needed in a really dark moment. I was so confused, knowing that I loved Carter but that I couldn't have his baby. And now this stranger was showing me more compassion than him.

Afterward, the nurses didn't say much. They left the room for a moment, and I assumed we were done, so I tried to stand up. As soon as I did, blood poured out of me, all over the floor. I nearly fainted—I cannot stand the sight of blood, it usually makes me black out. Honestly, I don't even know how I'm able to have a period every month and remain functioning.

Dazed, I stumbled outside into the waiting room, and the woman behind the front desk stood up, surprised.

"What are you doing? You're supposed to be lying down!"

I was delirious as the nurses helped me back into the surgery room and gave me the biggest sanitary pad I've ever seen in my life, just short of a diaper, to soak up the blood. Then, they put me in a recovery room, where I was given a juice box and orange slices to get my sugar back up. I was one hot mess, vomiting into a bowl, with my mom holding my hand, trying to keep me calm.

An hour later, I started feeling better. I put my clothes back on. Then, the strangest feeling hit me.

"Mom, I'm craving Arby's."

We hit the Arby's drive-through on our way home, and I ate, suddenly ravenous. It was all so surreal.

My grandma's celebration of life was taking place that evening. I didn't think there was any way I was going to make it, not after what I'd just been through. But I took a nap, and I woke up feeling like a different person. I felt okay, like I was back to normal. Which, in itself, added to the strangeness of the day. How could I feel normal after the day I'd just had? How can something so complex, like the creation of a baby, be so easy to cancel? Shouldn't I be in more pain? Physical torment would have made sense after what I'd just done. I'd been careless and stupid, and I felt guilty, not about my decision to have an abortion but that the process had been as quick and easy as it had been. These thoughts spun around my head as I dressed myself in all black and prepared to say goodbye to my grandmother.

My mom told me I should keep my abortion to myself; take it to my grave. But I've decided to share my story even though it may cause some of you to look at me differently, call me a "murderer," or send me hate mail. Some of you may even try to "cancel" me, or judge me, and that's okay, because that is your right. But I am a woman, and this is my body. No one will ever tell me what to do with it. I'm not the only one who chooses this option. I'm not the only one who deals with the guilt that comes with it. I *want* to talk about it. I want to challenge people and have debates about it. Too many people are frightened of uncomfortable conversations, and that's why we are where we are in this world today. Always fighting, judging, hating. Enough. I'm not ashamed of what I did. At the time, it was the best decision I could have made for my future, and I made it. I was fortunate to have support from my mom and the nurses at the clinic, but not everyone gets that same treatment. No woman should be made to feel less than, or ashamed, or guilty, for choosing that same path.

Grandma Mary-Lynn's wake took place at her beloved Mormon church. I stood up in front of our family and delivered a short eulogy. I told the congregation how Mary-Lynn had been known for calling me on the phone a lot and leaving me voice mails in her sweet, singsong voice. I said I liked to tell myself that the reason she called so much was because I was her favorite—but in reality, I knew she was concerned at how much of a rebel I was turning out to be and she wanted to make sure I was staying on the straight and narrow. Because that was the person she was. She cared. As I spoke, I felt overwhelmed by this sense of the cycle of life, how it had all converged upon this moment.

I knew she would never have agreed with the decision I took that day, and the procedure I had had, but she would have loved me just the same. Like she always had.

After the service ended, Sophia, my good friend, was waiting for me. I needed to tell her what I'd just gone through. The only private place was the kids' room, with Mormon puzzles and games where you choose things like "Go on a mission" and "Temple marriage." So I pulled her inside and told her I had some news.

"Dude, I had an abobo this morning," I whispered, using our code word for an abortion.

"What? I was out here nannying while my best friend's getting an abobo? What the fuck?" Sophia is very cynical and very funny. Hanging out with her is like being inside an episode of *Seinfeld* because she has the ability to take really intense stuff and make you laugh about it.

"God, you're just having a tough go, Lauren," she said. "Your grandmama dies, then you have an abobo, now we're at her wake. This is weird."

Sophia and I had come up with the word *abobo* back when we used to talk about the dangers of having unprotected sex—which was rare, for me. If there was one thing I was really good at, it was using condoms. If we're not in a committed relationship, then I don't know where your wiener has been, and the last thing any of us wanted was to have to get an abobo. Neither of us had ever had one before, and the word *abobo* was just girlfriend banter. Once I had one, I became less inclined to call it that because it is no joke. Whether you choose to have the baby, your body kicks into mother mode and you become a different human being, and afterward, because of the hormones, you can be emotionally affected.

I'll never judge anyone for having an abortion. I also understand why people might be against it. Either way, all women should have that choice. That's something I'm sure about. Because it happens, every day. Even women who say they don't agree with abortion have them sometimes, because that's their choice, and nobody's business but theirs.

"Wait, Carter doesn't know?" Sophia said, surprised.

"No. I can't get ahold of him."

I had been blowing up his phone all day, with no luck, but at that moment, my phone buzzed—Carter's timing, as always, was impeccable.

Hey, how are you?

I texted Carter back.

Everything's great. I'm at my grandma's wake and by the way, I had an abortion this morning. Just thought you should know.

Shut the fuck up, are you okay?

You know something? He *still* didn't call. And you know something else? I *still* didn't break up with him, although I probably should have. Instead, we fought about it for a really long time. We fought because I felt like he didn't care about what I had gone through and that he seemed incapable of understanding why I was upset about the way things had unfolded. Me getting pregnant, trying and failing to contact him, and then feeling so unable to communicate with him that I ended up going through it all by myself. Months later, I still wasn't over it, still trying to heal. I would break down, try to explain to Carter what I'd gone through, physically and emotionally. When the tears came, Carter would love on me, say how sorry he was, recognize that I'd gone through something hard. But what he gave me was never enough, because deep down, he didn't care the way I needed him to, when I needed him to.

Looking back now, I blame it all on age. I truly don't think Carter was a shitty guy; I think he was a young guy. There's a difference. He just didn't know how to handle what we were going through as a couple. And neither did I. We were just making it up as we went along. And before long, we settled back into our old routine.

For another year or so, texts and phone calls would go unanswered, and Carter would give me just enough to keep me hanging on before pulling away. It was exhausting, loving him. One day, after a hot shower, "Resentment" by Beyoncé on repeat, and a couple of vodka sodas, I made a bold move.

> Hi Carter. This isn't working for me anymore. I wish you all the best.

Then I blocked him.

I glammed. I pushed up the boobs, got my hair big, and covered myself in cocoa butter. Jamal, a football player at the University of Utah, was having a party. He'd let me know on many occasions that he was interested. I was going to try something I had never tried before—I was going to get under Jamal to get over Carter.

And this time, you better believe I used protection.

chapter seven

TRUE ROMANCE

*I*T WAS DECEMBER 2015, the fourth episode of my first season had just aired, and I was working a hostess shift at SUR because that was my job now. We weren't being filmed—*Vanderpump* had wrapped filming for that season—but life was feeling pretty perfect. I was over Carter. The *Vanderpump* fans were going nuts about Lala (haters and stans alike). I felt like things were on the up and up.

In the middle of my shift, two movie-industry types dressed in black came up to me at the hostess stand, wanting a table. The restaurant was packed, and they didn't have a reservation. Their timing couldn't have been worse. The boss guy saw someone he knew at a table and went to say hello to them. As he did, I tried to find an open table in the system, while making small talk with the assistant, who mentioned he was a huge fan of the show. He said his name was Sam.

"Thank you, that's so nice of you to say, Sam," I said, smiling. I always made a point to be extra sweet to any diners who were fans of *Vanderpump*.

He told me his boss was a film producer. In Hollywood, everyone and their aunt is a "producer" or a "screenwriter" making a "film," so I didn't think too much of it. But I did casually mention I had studied acting before getting on *Vanderpump*, because it never hurts to put yourself out there, right? This information seemed to interest the assistant, and he asked me if I had a manager.

"Sure," I said. "Go to my Instagram. My manager's info is on there."

The next day my manager, Rob, called me and said, "Great news, Lala. I got an email from Randall Emmett's office this morning about a casting. His assistant said he met you last night?"

"Randall Emmett? Who's Randall Emmett?"

"You need to look him up right now, Lala."

I went on the Internet and typed in the name. Movie credit after movie credit after movie credit. He'd produced movies starring Mark Wahlberg, Salma Hayek, Sylvester Stallone, Snoop—this guy was super legit. Could it be that Sam, the nice assistant guy and *Vanderpump* stan, had convinced Randall, his big-shot boss, that I deserved an audition for a part in one of their upcoming movies?

A few days later, Rob and I went to the Beverly Hills offices of Randall's film company, Emmett Furla Films, the iconic building formally known as Suge Knight's office. The audition was for a supporting role in a movie called *The Row*, about a killer who goes on a rampage in a sorority house—super fun and campy.

My palms were sweating—I knew this wasn't just some meet and greet where I could be Lala. I had to be Lauryn Kent, the aspiring actress. I had the script in my hand and had read my scenes over and over. I was trippin'.

We were escorted into an office, where Randall sat behind his desk, like a boss. The atmosphere was formal, and I kept my poise, trying to behave as though I did this kind of thing every day.

Sam, the assistant, smiled as he handed me sides (brief scenes from a script, used in auditions), and I read the part of Celeste Aster for Randall and the director, Matty.

I guess I crushed it because a few days later, I got a callback. Immediately after, they told me I'd booked the job. I couldn't believe this was happening. I had booked my first real job in Hollywood. Which was exciting enough, but imagine my surprise when Sam called my manager a few days later to say Matty wanted me to play the part of Riley Cole instead—the lead.

I couldn't believe that after all those years of trying and dreaming, *Vanderpump* really had opened up the doors I'd been banging on all these years. The little girl who'd signed the contract saying "I, Lauren Burningham, will not stop until I am in the movies" was very proud of me, I knew that. She was already imagining how she'd describe this moment for her *E! True Hollywood Story*.

Rob and I arranged to meet Randall at Mr Chow, a high-end restaurant in Beverly Hills, to discuss the role over lunch. I knew about Mr Chow because it was in one of the lyrics of "Don't Worry" by Chingy, featuring Janet Jackson. This was literally the most bougie thing I had ever done—business lunch at Mr Chow—I needed to be professional AF. No alcohol for Lala—I'd stick to water, and hold off on cursing. I'd be *classy*.

Rob and I arrived at the restaurant, sat at our table, and waited for Randall. As soon as he arrived, he put us all at ease with his upbeat energy. He ordered their vegetable dumplings, chicken satay, and the lettuce wraps—to this day, that's what he always orders there, because he's a creature of habit.

We started bumping gums (Lala-speak for "chatting"), and the conversation flowed effortlessly as Randall filled us in on his résumé and how he got started, and I told him how I moved to LA to become an actress and how I landed on a reality show. He was friendly, relaxed, and congratulated me on making a wonderful impression on the director, who thought I was perfect for the role.

We discussed where *The Row* would shoot and when, making sure there was no conflict with *Vanderpump Rules*, and conversation between Randall and I was so fun I actually forgot that my manager was still there. Something about Randall's energy, his mannerisms. I was shook by how attracted I was to him because he was so different from the guys I had dated in the past. There was something about him that felt intriguing. Whatever it was, it gave me butterflies.

Randall picked up the tab, and outside, gave the valet guy his ticket for his whip while Rob, who didn't valet, went to get his car. Randall told me he was headed to the Sundance Film Festival in a couple of days—Sundance takes place in Park City, Utah, a forty-minute drive from my house in SLC. I told Randall I'd had my fair share of fun at Sundance over the years, back when I would work celebrity lounges, handing out goody bags and cocktails to famous people. I'd usually catch a good buzz, and my little brother, Easton, would pick me up, sauced, at the end of the night I told Randall about my experiences at the festival and the films I'd seen there. I had always dreamed about going there not to work a party, but as an actress. Randall was supportive and assured me that day would come for me, very soon. (And, he was right. In 2020, I attended Sundance to promote a film I was in.)

We had a table read scheduled for after Sundance, but Randall had to pull out, because he'd caught a terrible flu that was going around Park City. We decided to reschedule the read, but then, I got sick, too, and couldn't make it. Damn flu season. I sent Randall and assistant Sam an email explaining I was as sick as a dog, and that afternoon, a crate of organic cold-pressed juices arrived at my apartment, along with several DVDs of movies Emmett Furla had produced. I decided to watch *Everest* that night, remembering my dad had talked about it once, saying he wanted to see it. It was so surreal to me that I was going to be the star of a movie made by the same guy who made movies my dad talked about.

Randall or someone from his office checked in every day, to see how I was feeling, and did I need anything. I was so touched by how thoughtful they were. When I got well again, and we finally had our meeting, I asked Randall for his card, and we began a text thread that I still treasure. It wasn't flirty—we never said anything cheesy to each other, like "You're so hot," rather, we took a genuine interest in each other's days. And he kept up with the juices, a whole boxful, once a week for me and my new roommate.

She was loving it. "These are like twelve dollars a bottle; this is dope."

On a friend's birthday, she decided she wanted to go to a super popular place called the Bungalow in Santa Monica at the last minute. It was a weekend, and I knew it was going to be next to impossible getting a table on such short notice. I texted Randall, "Hey, do you know anybody over at the Bungalow who can get us a table? There's a group of us." I knew that if anyone could hook us up, it would be him, because everyone in town seemed to know him.

Rand texted me back, "Go right now, ask for the GM, and tell him I sent you." I did what he said, and when we showed up, the GM came out, opened the rope, and walked us all inside. He didn't ask us for a credit card, just brought out bottles of alcohol and a whole ton of food. Randall had taken care of all of it. I wondered, *Does he do this kind of stuff for everybody?* Because I had never been treated with such kindness and generosity before. By this point, Sam and I were buddies, so I asked him, "Does he do this kind of stuff for everybody?" He told me Randall was known for taking care of anyone working on a movie with him. I'll admit, I was a little disappointed. I had a crush on Randall, and part of me hoped that maybe he thought I was special. Not long after, I started to realize that yes, he did.

Whenever there was a new version of the script, Sam would deliver it by hand to my apartment. One day, along with the latest draft, came an army-green Chanel Boy bag and Christian Louboutin fringe booties. I was blown away, and my heart fluttered. *Was he into me the way I was into him?* I wasn't used to a dude treating me like a queen. It had always been all words and no actions with other men I had spent time with. I now know that gifts are Randall's way of showing he loves you and cares for you, because he's the kind of guy who derives genuine pleasure from making people feel special. Randall was showing me that he liked me, without having to say the words.

About three months after Randall and I met, Rob, my manager, called to tell me that *Watch What Happens Live* wanted to have me back on the show. This was unexpected, considering last time I'd appeared on *WWHL*, my drunk ass had been named Jackhole of the Week. But now they wanted Lala back, and I leapt at the chance. Bravo booked me on a flight to New York the next day; and I happened to know that Randall was there in New York. I got so excited! It felt like the universe was trying to tell me something.

I casually mentioned to Randall that I was going to be in New York, and he casually invited me and my hair and makeup team, who were flying out with me, to join him for a drink after we shot *WWHL*. I really liked this guy, and couldn't wait to hang out socially with him. My mother, however, wasn't having it.

"Lauren, absolutely not," she said. "He is a film producer; you want to be in film. No cocktails together, especially if you have feelings for him. You should keep it professional with this guy." It's very rare that I ignore my mother's advice, because she's nearly always right about everything. But this time, I didn't listen to my mother, because my gut was telling me I should go. And my instinct has never let me down.

I thought about what my father had told me to do after my drunken performance last time I went to New York to appear on *Watch What Happens Live*. Following my dad's advice to apologize had almost certainly paved the way for me to be invited back, and now here I was, about to meet Randall in New York. Coincidence? I don't know—it all felt like destiny to me, somehow.

My second appearance on *WWHL* went without a hitch. I was a very good girl. I allowed myself one vodka soda, I didn't cuss, and everyone had fun. They had played it safe this time and prerecorded the show, just in case. Afterward, I was thanked for being a great guest on a successful episode of *WWHL*. Andy was much warmer to me this time. I can't remember who the Jackhole of the Week was, but I am 100 percent certain it wasn't me.

When I left the building that *WWHL* films in, a kid came up to me, wanting to take a picture—it was the same boy from last time, there with his mom. This time, I was clearheaded enough to ask him some questions about himself. He opened up and told me that watching me on TV had helped him stand up to people and behave with more confidence. My heart melted right then and there on that sidewalk in Manhattan. This was already shaping up to be a perfect weekend.

I called Randall to let him know I was finished and could meet up. I had my hair and makeup team with me, and Madison, who was now living in New York. Randall asked if we wanted a quiet atmosphere for dinner or something more lively.

"Lively!" I said, thinking, *I've been pretty much sober all day. I wanna get it poppin'.*

Randall said we should meet him at a place called Tao. When we arrived, he was waiting at a table in the middle of the room on the bottom level of the restaurant. We sat down, ordered, and the conversation flowed easily, just like it had at his office, at Mr Chow, and in every text and phone conversation we'd ever had. At some point in the night, during a story he was telling, I felt compelled to touch him. It felt like the most natural thing in the world. Underneath the table, I took his hand and felt his hand squeezing mine back. My heart was pounding. I'd never felt like this about anyone before.

We went on to Tao nightclub, and there, we kissed for the first time. I didn't end up using my hotel room that night. I stayed with him in his. Yes, I let Randall hit it on the first date, although if you break it down, that first date had been several months, several hundred text conversations, and a lot of bottled up feelings in the making. Once those feelings were out, there was no way to put them back in again.

When we slept together, every part of me was feeling something, because I was ready, and because I knew what I wanted—and that was more than just the fun of casual sex. I had been with guys who had treated me wrong, but now I knew I had finally found someone who was going to be different. Because we had a foundation of friendship, we had a deeper connection from the start and were in tune with each other on every level. I think that's why the physical side of things was so powerful, unlike anything I'd ever experienced. There was trust. And when you trust, anything is possible. Even now, I'm so emotionally connected to Rand that sex with him remains the best sex I've ever had.

Later that night, after having sex for the first time, I was in the bathtub in Rand's hotel room with the bathroom door open because I felt that comfortable and relaxed around him. I decided to remove all my makeup, which surprised even me—I'm the girl who'd prep a "nighttime makeup" bag whenever I went to see Carter, who'd never, ever seen me completely fresh-faced. Randall walked into the bathroom as I was bathing, looked at me, and said, "You're the most beautiful person I've ever seen." He was seeing me at my most naked and vulnerable, and for the first time in my entire life, I felt completely safe with a man. Wanted, and like I was good enough. That night, I fell in love with Randall. That night, we became inseparable. We both knew this was something real.

Carter, though, was still calling me, begging to see me, and I had to figure out how to explain to him that I was in love with someone else now. Carter and I had so much history. I'd gotten pregnant by him; it felt like we'd gone to hell and back. But I knew I'd be stupid to go back to him after everything that relationship had put me through.

One night, Randall and I were in bed after a night out, pretty drunk, and Carter called, saying he wanted to get back together with me. I had a long, very serious conversation with him, with Randall lying by my side. The following morning, Rand turned to me, looking worried, and asked me, "So you think you're going to get back together with that guy?"

"What guy?"

"You had a phone call with your ex last night, Lala."

"I did?"

Nope. Didn't even remember.

Then, a text message from Carter popped up on my phone.

So, did you make your decision?

I'm sorry, Carter . . . . I've met someone else.

And that was that. I was free. I felt truly happy, lying in the arms of this guy who was so different from any other I'd ever been with.

Before I met Rand, I always thought I had a "type," but now I realize how limiting that idea can be. Only dating one type of person means you're putting yourself and your heart in a box, while excluding a million and one people out there who could be bringing you everything you deserve in a relationship, if only you'd let them.

That's why I tell people, don't worry about checking boxes on some list when you're dating. Don't prioritize finding someone who is exactly your "type." Instead, try looking for someone who cherishes you, heart and soul. Someone who cares about how you feel and your outlook on life. Make that your type, and let the rest follow. These days, you could put my old "type" in front of me and I wouldn't even notice, because I'm with a man who I find sexy, attractive, and who I have mad chemistry with—in the bed and out of it.

I always ask Randall *why me?* I'm rough around the edges; I'm hardheaded; I'm high-strung—but he explains that as far as he's concerned, I'm a badass, and he loves every little part of me, the good and the not so good. He's my lover and my best friend, and he has been there, by my side, during the darkest days of my existence. I had no idea when we got together just how much I'd need him later on down the line.

Randall and I had been together a year and a half before he introduced me to his kids, London and Rylee. I was happy to wait until the time was right—I knew that if my parents had ever separated, my dad wouldn't have brought anyone around me and my brother until he was sure they were going to be a constant in our lives. Kids are the most innocent, beautiful souls, and it is our job to provide them with consistency and protection so that, one day, they can go into the big, bad world and take it on like champs, always knowing they have a safe place at home.

When the time came, Randall said, "I'm going to have a barbecue this weekend, and you can come as my 'friend.'"

I thought it was a brilliant idea. I brought a dozen red velvet cupcakes from Sprinkles for the kids, which single-handedly made me London and Rylee's favorite human being at the barbecue. That, and swimming with them until I was pruned.

I was "Daddy's friend" for a while. I would only come around for an hour or two when he had his kids over—Randall was separated from his ex-wife and going through a divorce, and I thought it was important to make sure they had time alone with their dad as they adjusted to their parents living apart. The girls, however, demanded my presence fairly often. They wanted Lala to sleep over, Lala to come over, and often, I'd pick up my phone to hear their little voices on the other end, wanting to have a chat.

London, Rylee, and I became the Three Musketeers. Rylee would say, "It's girl time, no boy time," to her dad when we had sleepovers, and the three of us would sleep in the main bedroom and put Randall in the guest room. We are a tight little girl squad.

After a while, Randall took them to the park for a daddy-daughter picnic and asked them what they thought about Daddy asking Lala to be his girlfriend.

"Yeah! You should ask her!" they said.

"I should?! Do you think she'll say yes?"

"Yes, she will for sure say yes."

Just like that, I was approved by the two most important ladies in Randall's life, and his babies became my babies, and I vowed to protect them and love them like the ultimate bonus mom. I held them when they cried, put them in check when they acted up, and not long ago, I gifted them my favorite Lee Middleton dolls from when I was a kid, still pristine in the original boxes. That's how much I love those girls.

Some people say that when you sleep with someone on the first date, you run the risk of making it a one-and-done, and that may be. But for Rand and I, the opposite was true. And when the time came for Dad to ask Lala to be his wife, Randall would once again ask for his daughters' approval. Luckily for me, they said yes.

chapter eight

PRIVATE JETS AND GUCCI SLIDES

ANY OF YOU WATCHED the episode of *Vanderpump Rules* where I told Stassi how Randall gave me a Range Rover after the first night we slept together in New York. That's when "gold-digging whore" became a pretty standard insult thrown at me, and watching the episode, I can totally see how people jumped to this (inaccurate) conclusion about the dynamic between Randall and me. To those who continue to hate, I will say this: Wouldn't *you* take a free car if someone offered it to you? If you answer no, you're either lying or you've already got a lot of cars. Anyway, I'm going to tell you exactly how things went down, because sometimes it's impossible for the whole story to be told on TV.

The morning after Randall and I hooked up, we were in bed in his hotel room in New York, just waking up, when he turned to me and asked, "Do you want a Range Rover?"

I was too hungover to really take in what he was saying.

"Like, the car?"

"Yeah."

"Uh. Yeah. I would love that, of course."

"Okay," he said. "I'll have it dropped off to your apartment right now. What's your address?"

I sat up in the bed and looked at him.

"Are you being for real?"

"Yeah!"

"Randall, I already have a car. . . ."

"Yeah, but it's probably not nice."

"Actually, it is nice. I have a BMW 3 Series." I had had that car for a while; it was my second BMW. My first, which I'd bought with savings, had gotten smashed into, and with the insurance payout, I upgraded to a sexier model.

"Oh, that is a nice car. Well, does your mom need a car?"

"Maybe? She doesn't need one, but she might want one."

"Let's give her your car, and you take the Range Rover. Okay?"

Randall really is a one-man gifting suite.

We called my mom together and put her on speaker, and I asked her if she wanted my BMW because Randall was going to give me a new car.

"Yes, uh, of course I would love that," she said, a slightly confused tone in her voice. I think she thought we were being silly.

Randall said, "Okay. We're flat-bedding the BMW from LA to you in Salt Lake City today." He was so matter-of-fact and efficient, I almost didn't believe he was for real. But it was.

Later that day, I asked my roommate back at the Ho Palace if there was a Range Rover in the driveway.

"Yup," she said. Then she took a picture and sent it to me.

Mama got the BMW, and I got the Range Rover, which worked out great for both of us.

Maybe you've heard of the 5 Love Languages? It's a theory about how all of us express love in certain ways. It can be through words of affirmation, acts of service, receiving gifts, quality time, physical touch. (Being Santa Claus is the sixth love language, which Randall invented.)

For me, gifts are actually very low on the totem pole; I'm much more about words of affirmation and touch. That being said, I am never going to turn down a Chanel bag, and nor is any other woman on this planet. I always say, people who criticize you for accepting a Chanel bag are probably not getting very many Chanel bags sent to them. But after a while of hearing the insults being thrown at me, I did have to take a long look in the mirror and question myself. "*Are* you a gold-digging whore, Lala?" Even though I knew the answer—a categorical no—my cast members and haters were saying it so often, I had started second-guessing myself.

Thanks to my Mormon overexposure, I'm allergic to passing those kinds of judgments, and that's why I'll never knock a real-life gold digger. I respect anybody who's out there doing what they need to do to make a dollar. Take advantage of the opportunities presented to you in life. My job is not to judge you for doing what you need to do. If your lifestyle doesn't directly affect me, get it how you live, boo. I'll never knock a female hustle. I wish that I could say, "You know what, I'm going to date for money to make sure I'm taken care of." That would make life way less complicated. Unfortunately, I have to be emotionally connected and sexually connected with someone in order to be in a relationship.

If you get involved with a rich person and you're with them because they're wealthy, I just hope that you have enough respect for that person to not leave *them* high and dry at any point. Be kind to yourself, be kind to others, and get what you need. If you guys are happy together, if you're a hot bombshell, and they've got cash, then you're both benefiting from what the other can offer. Fair trade.

Some people were shocked when I told them that Randall and I were getting a prenup before we married. But I'm all about it. In fact, I told Randall that if the prenup wasn't fully completed before we walked down the aisle, we would have to postpone our wedding. I want to put his mind at ease, that if things don't work out, I have no intention of taking away what he has worked so hard for. My fiancé has been building his company since I was five years old, and went from sleeping on people's couches to creating this incredible business. And that's his.

Truthfully, I wanted the prenup, too. I'm only thirty years old yet, and Give Them Lala, the brand I have built and continue to grow daily, is special to me. I have worked hard to get to where I am, and I know one day Give Them Lala will become an empire. And when it does, I want to make sure it is protected if my marriage to Randall were to fall apart.

That long look I took in the mirror? What it told me was that I'm not with Randall for any other reason than love because, let's be real, if I *were* a gold digger, I'd be the best damn gold digger out there. I'd be with the billionaire, honey. I'd be on an island somewhere, yachting every other day. And if I were a whore—which I define as a person who gets paid to have sex—I'd be charging top dollar. I'd be the most expensive whore you've ever met.

But I'm not. I'm with Randall because I've never had anybody take care of my heart and soul the way that he has. And to see the way that he took my family in, and the way he loved them from day one, that was huge for me. My family is my world, and Randall understands that sometimes they might come and stay for weeks on end. Most dudes would say, "This is weird, you need to separate a little bit, cut the cord already." But Randall's all "Bring it on, and PS, let's mail your mom a car."

I remember watching an interview in which Tupac Shakur talked about how it doesn't make sense that some people are billionaires, while others are out there, homeless and starving. And I agree. If we're talking real life, I want to talk about how it makes zero sense that so many people are living in poverty, struggling to feed their kids, living on food stamps when there are people out there who are worth hundreds of millions of dollars, into the billion-dollar range. How is that happening in the world?

It's happening because our society pays people who dribble balls more than it pays schoolteachers, and because our leaders care more about who's bringing in the most cash instead of the education of our children. They *pretend* that they care, but if they really did, they would make damn sure that every child was getting the level of schooling that they need, and we would be paying those teachers a lot of money, because those kids are the future of our fucked-up world.

For me, that just tells me that our country is built on greed. I mean, think about how much money people are making off me from acting like a damn fool on television. It's insane. So, I may make jokes about Gucci slides and private jets—but no, flying commercial doesn't really give me anxiety. I just say that stuff to get a rise out of people on reality television, because that's the shit Lala says. Off camera, I know that's not what life's about.

Yes, being on a private plane is great because there's no security, or luggage restrictions, or showing up three hours early. But before meeting Randall, I had only flown on a private jet once, and that's because my friend's dad was dating a private-jet flight attendant and there was an empty G4 going to Seattle, so we hopped on. As for designer bags, I inherited some from my grandmother, but I had never experienced going into a luxury store and dropping money on one until much later. So I talk a good game because it's fun for TV—we have established I spew a lot of bullshit and I enjoy getting a good rise out of people: that's who Lala is. But the Lala you don't see knows the difference between real life and baller life, because she's lived them both. She's seen the highs that money can bring and the devastation when it's suddenly taken away, because that's what happened to my family.

Both my grandparents on my dad's side worked in education. My grandpa Rulon was a school principal, and my grandma Mary-Lynn was a teacher. On their combined salaries, and with four kids to raise, they had to get used to living pretty lean, making each dollar stretch. My dad told me that every summer before the school year started, my grandparents would sit the kids down and put out all the money they had on a table and sort it into envelopes. One envelope was for books, one envelope was so they each had one new outfit for the school year. And so on. Every paycheck that came in, they did the same. They separated it into envelopes, in front of the kids.

Growing up with envelopes made my dad determined to make

a different life for his family. He wanted to live differently, and from a young age, he was an entrepreneur. As a young kid, he started a lawn-mowing company, cutting everyone's grass in the neighborhood each summer. After that, he started a carpet-cleaning business. Then he started a real-estate development business, Spectrum Development, with his brother, and together they started building homes in Salt Lake. I remember the company started out in a really small office. They started building bigger and grander houses, for clients from New York, Dubai, and Los Angeles. The housing boom was in full swing, and my dad was cashing in.

One day, we went to his new office, and it was just spectacular. My dad showed me these models of the homes he was building in subdivisions. He had all of this land in Deer Valley and was building these monstrosities that were tens of thousands of square feet. I loved those little models, I wished my Barbies and Polly Pockets could play in them.

My dad built our house from the ground up, and it was impeccably done, gorgeous. It sat at the back of a cul-de-sac. At the front, a giant window looked into the living room with a beautiful baby grand piano that my parents had bought for me when I decided to take on piano lessons, although I was famous for starting an instrument and quickly giving it up.

There was a giant chandelier in the entryway. The backyard was a great size, and I had an epic play palace with swings, monkey bars, a volleyball net, and a picnic area. My dad made Easton a putting green in the backyard, with flags. Easton and I had a giant playroom with vaulted ceilings and a balcony that I later turned into my bedroom, where my dad built me my first walk-in closet. There was a workout room, and our basement had its own kitchen, a pool table, a Ping-Pong table, and a big-screen TV. That's where all the little heathens would hang out on the weekends. Our house was amazing, and our lifestyle was very comfortable.

Each year, me and my brother, and Madison, Olivia, and Danielle would go with our parents and their friends to a holiday house in Newport Beach for these over-the-top vacations, where we didn't flinch at ordering a $17 virgin pina colada at the Ritz-Carlton pool. Love and togetherness was all my family needed to be happy, but having money in those days sure made life fun, for as long as it lasted, which wasn't as long as we thought it would.

From age zero until I was eighteen, our lives were perfect and we wanted for nothing, then in 2008, the housing market tanked, and America entered the Great Recession. I started overhearing my parents fighting about finances. Like I said before, I was always very in tune with people's energy and their emotions, and I could sense something was wrong, even though they didn't sit me down and say, "This is serious, we're having money issues." There was so much stress in our household; the air was thick with it all the time, and I felt a pressure I was unfamiliar with. I knew things were messed up when one day, I was sitting on the stairs, and my mom walked in the door, sobbing, saying, "This is bad. This is really bad."

I tried comforting her. I drove her up to Park City, bought her lunch at Cafe Rio, a local Mexican restaurant obsession, and told her, "Money will come and go. We have to stay strong as a family." I was only a senior in high school, and I didn't really know what to say, but I wanted to try and help her feel better. Most of all, I wanted to remind my dad how proud I was of him and let him know we weren't looking at him any differently than before, just because his business was tanking. To me, my dad was incredible whether we were doing well financially or not, and I needed him to know that, because it was obvious how stressed and sad all this was making him. With his health being so up and down over the years, I didn't want this stress further deteriorating his body.

I started writing handwritten letters to my dad and leaving them by his bathroom sink so that he would see them in the morning. They were always long, and started with "To the most amazing dad." Then I would write out something that made him feel special, like, "What you've provided for us is incredible. You've given me the best life in the world. I hope you go out there and kill it today and know how amazing you are. I love you so much." Things that communicated that we were proud of him, no matter what. Anytime I would leave a letter for him, he would come into my room, sit on my bed, and kiss me on the forehead. I would pretend to be asleep, knowing that he was feeling emotional.

I begged my parents to sell our house. It was a large home, very beautiful, and my mom had decorated it to the nines—but I wanted out so badly, because I didn't want to hear them fighting about having to pay the mortgage anymore. "Put us in a freaking cracker box somewhere so that we can just enjoy our life!" I'd say. Having witnessed so much fighting over money in those times, I realized that money ain't shit. I didn't care about it. To this day, the only thing I want in my life is to be able to be someone's teammate and make things work, because if we're healthy and happy living in a box, then that's where I want to be. But my dad couldn't bring himself to let go of our home. I recently found out that he cried to Easton one day and said, "I can't sell this house because it reminds me of my accomplishments." That house was a huge financial burden, but in a way it was his identity. He had built that house for us and was going to cling to it come hell or high water.

I could see my dad's heart sink when my mom started suggesting jobs—any job would do, a plethora of random jobs. She suggested he work at the local movie theater, where her friend's husband, who had also been affected by the recession, was working. But my dad was too proud. A year ago he had been building $10 million homes; now his wife was asking if he wanted to rip tickets at a movie theater. He tried to stay positive while desperately searching for alternative sources of income.

"Everything's going to be fine, I've got irons in the fire," he'd say. He started looking into a bunch of multilevel marketing, pyramid schemes (these are big in Utah), because he was great at selling. He was trustworthy and had a sparkle in his eyes that people were drawn to . . . but I saw that sparkle begin to fade after a while.

I never in a million years thought I'd hear my dad ask me to fill his car up with gas so that he could go out and try to make a dollar. But that's what wound up happening, and every time he would ask, I could tell how embarrassed he was. I never thought twice about it, though. That was where we were at for a while. He made me promise not to tell Mom, so we kept it a secret. I paid to register all the family's cars, going down to Jiffy Lube to get them inspected and paying $180 per car with the money I was earning from the little modeling gigs I was getting. I was fine with that. I kept thinking how my dad had provided me with such an incredible lifestyle up until that point. If he needed his cars registered, I could do that.

With cash so tight, I would take any job that was offered to me. I dressed in a nude body suit for an acupuncture class so the doctor could place sticky Velcro dots on my body in front of his students, like a live doll—$200 for seven hours. I was a sock model at an outdoor sports convention, working a booth that was promoting this new amazing fabric for mountaineering footwear. People would walk by, and I'd have to tell them how amazing these socks were, how warm they keep your feet. I'd stick my foot under a hot lamp, then stick it into a refrigerated area to demonstrate that these socks kept your toes the perfect temperature, no matter what.

I modeled prom dresses, but because I was short for a model, they had to put me in stripper heels to make me look like I was five ten. I modeled these dresses for seven hours straight, strapped in so tight that I became dizzy, trying to stand straight but not lock my knees up in those heels. They paid me $700 a day, and I'd give a portion of it to the family. I'm sure we needed more than what I was giving, but I did what I could. I had been a saver since I started working at twelve, and it felt good to be able to contribute. My mom was working, and Easton got a job at a golf course. It was all hands on deck. We were a team. My mom's mother had died a decade prior and left her a large inheritance, which saved our asses in the end and wound up being what we lived off. That's how we were able to keep the house.

A lot of people say you should hide money problems from your kids. Even my mom says she wishes she could have hidden it from us better, but I'm glad she didn't. I saw real life happen. I saw my parents argue, but more important, I saw them stick together. I learned so much from both of them during this period—seeing my dad thrive and lose everything, then watching my mom stand by his side through all of it. Even though we went from having not a care in the world to being burdened with financial issues we would never recover from, we had each other, and we felt safe.

That's why I have the relationship with money that I do. I've seen money come and go so quickly, that for me to base my relationship off a dollar number seems silly. My mom was nineteen years old when she met my dad, and she was with him during his highest highs and his lowest lows. That, for me, has been one of the most inspiring things in my life. I want to do that for someone. I want my partner to know that if he ever couldn't handle our life financially, he has me to lean back on. Because, believe it or not, I make money, too.

After the recession, my father never really got back to being his old self. But there were moments, every once in a while, when he was in his element and having a good time, and the sparkle would return. I remember wanting to be a sponge in those moments, because they were becoming so few and far between. I wanted to bottle those moments up and remember them, and make them last forever.

chapter nine

HOME-WRECKING WHORES HAVE FEELINGS, TOO

*A*FTER MINE AND RANDALL'S first night together in New York, we were gone for three months. It was like some wild, perfect honeymoon. We flew to Miami, to the Bahamas, back to New York for work, then to Utah to meet my family, and back to Miami. He told his parents about me and would call me when he was at dinner with them. We were madly in love, and it was hard not to yell from the rooftops that I had fallen for this man, who was twenty years older than me and lived in California, on a hill, just like the psychic in Aspen had told me.

After those first three months together, zipping around in the G5 to movie sets, poppin' bottles on yachts, falling in love, we hit our first real bump in the road. While he and his soon-to-be ex-wife, from whom he was separated, were still finalizing their divorce, Randall thought it best we keep our relationship quiet. I hated the idea. When I'm in love, I am out and proud with my relationship. I don't like eating in back rooms and not being able to post selfies with my honey. It sucked. I'd never been married or divorced before, so I found it hard to understand.

Randall and I would get heated about it, as I started feeling more and more resentful that we couldn't just openly make out and hold hands around town like a normal couple. It took a lot of work and babying from Randall, but eventually, I put my ego aside and tried to understand what he was saying. Just be patient, Lala. Just let it be. Reluctantly, I decided the best way to announce my love to the world would be a little tattoo on my arm that read R.E. For now, that would have to be enough.

Being with Randall was unlike any other dating experience I'd ever had. He was a grown-ass man, not a boy still figuring himself out. He was successful, and a doting father to two girls, and had adult AF baggage that made my prior relationships look like child's play. I was starting to realize that when you're with a real man, who has a real history and kids, things can get complicated. But I will say this—I've never doubted Randall's integrity, nor his love for me. Which is kind of a miracle in the business we're in. To this day, when girls send him DMs, saying, "I'll do this nasty thing for you, if you put me in your movie, or buy me these shoes," he shows me those messages, and we laugh. Then he asks to see my in-box, too, in case I'm getting hit up by guys. Which never really happens. Only about 12 percent of the people who follow me are heterosexual males, and I can't remember the last time a straight man slid into my DMs and told me I was hot—it's all females, gay guys, and trans babes in my in-box, all of them fabulous.

With Randall, I never have that pit in my stomach, that female intuition sending me alarm bells. The second that happens, I'll know that Randall and I shouldn't be together. I hope it never does. He's my best friend. I go to the office with him every day. He always wants me to come to boys' night, and I have to shove him out the door so he can go have time with his friends. Even then, he's calling and texting to check in. He's devoted, as am I. Neither of us put up with shit from anyone, and he knows I have a lot of self-respect. No amount of money in this world will ever keep me with someone I can't trust.

Randall and I intended to continue keeping things nice and low-key until his divorce was behind him, then we could all move on with our lives, without any drama. Right? *Wrong.* Hollywood is one small, vicious gossip mill, and before long, the whole town knew I was with Randall, and they were coming for me with pitchforks. And the person I could thank for that was Katie Maloney, my castmate and archnemesis at the time. Here's how the dominoes collapsed.

An actor working on one of Randall's movies had brought his wife to a barbecue that Katie happened to be at. Season five was about to start shooting, and Katie, who thought I was the antichrist at the time, was gossiping about me. She mentioned that I had just gotten a new tattoo on my arm of *R.E.*, and this actor's wife spilled the tea.

"Yeah, she's with *Randall Emmett*! My husband just shot a movie with him, and Lala was there on set for, like, three weeks straight. Oh, and by the way, he's *married*."

Katie, Kristen, and Stassi had already made my life misery on season four, so you can bet Katie wasted no time sharing the gossip with the whole cast, at which point I went from being a mere "gold-digging whore" to a "home-wrecking whore," wantonly destroying the lives of a beautiful, happily married couple. An untrue story, of course, but they neither knew, nor cared to check with me.

FML.

Since I was blissfully unaware that any of this was coming down the pipe, Randall and I had come up with a plan to explain to the cast of *Vanderpump* why I was no longer ho-phasing my little heart out—I was going to pretend that I was in a relationship with an athlete who lived in Long Beach and whose mom was my good friend. We invented a whole backstory for this guy, and I memorized it perfectly. At the time I felt so clever, lying on reality TV, treating the whole thing like an acting job. On season five, I would just have to pretend to be myself. My "performance" would be short-lived.

On *Vanderpump*, cast members never know what's going to happen during the season. Instead, the producers sit us all down individually for a long meeting before each season starts shooting and ask us what's been going on in our lives and what we've heard about other cast members' lives, searching for the real-life drama that can be massaged into good TV. Even the couples on the show meet with the producers separately, and it's like a therapy session. No topic is off-limits. I love the producers, but they're also our enemies because it's their job to make us talk about real issues we don't want to talk about. And you can guarantee we will be encouraged to deal with those issues.

The time came for my meeting with the producers, at a restaurant on Sunset Boulevard. I was excited to serve a second season of Lala to the fans. The *Vanderpump* showrunner smiled at me as I sat down for my interview. "Well, I guess you already know what this season is going to entail for you."

I shook my head. "What are you talking about?"

"What does that tattoo on your arm stand for, Lala?" He was looking at the *R.E.* on the inside of my arm.

Randall and I had already figured this one out. "Oh, it's for my grandparents, Robert and Elyse."

He raised his eyebrows. "Well, I'm hearing something else, and I just wanted to give you the heads-up that you and Randall Emmett are going to be very much talked about on season five."

Fuck, fuck, FUCK.

I told him he had it all wrong. That I had a new Long Beach babe who was camera shy, quiet, and worked very long hours, so unfortunately, we wouldn't be seeing much of him. I knew there was no way Randall would allow his private life, and the privacy of his daughters, to be a topic of discussion on this season of *Vanderpump Rules*, so I denied, denied, denied, and said it was all just idle gossip, Katie being mean because she wasn't getting laid. But the producer didn't fall for it.

I walked out of the meeting in a daze and called Randall.

"We're in trouble, boo," I said. "They know everything."

We started filming two weeks later. Cast members asked me incessantly who I was dating, and I stuck to my guns. I said I was with an athlete whose mom lives in Long Beach, and that's where I went on the weekends. My R.E. tattoo was my grandparents' initials. Season five, I was heavy on lying. But here's the problem; I love to act, but I have never been very good at lying. And now I was under a lot of pressure to maintain this facade, not for me, but for the well-being of Randall's family that was going through a delicate time. While the rumors about me swirled, the word *home-wrecker* kept being thrown around by Katie, Stassi, and Kristen. Something inside me snapped. I hated this. I was so angry and felt ambushed. The only way I knew how to handle those feelings was to numb them.

My *Vanderpump* call times ranged anywhere between 10:00 a.m. and 10:00 p.m., into the wee hours of the night. Dreading each day of filming, I started drinking at home while I was getting ready, a little Dutch courage. Then once I got to the filming location, I would have more drinks there. For the entirety of shooting, I would drink all day, and through the night, the partying would continue. Shoots could end at 2:00 a.m. I was pretty young, so hangovers were nothing, and I figured the best way to handle them was to just keep drinking. That was my go-to move—wake up, pop my Advil with my coffee, have a couple of vodka sodas, then head to SUR and go toes with whatever bitch was coming for me that day. As long as I was drunk, I could handle it. As long as I was drunk, I could give as good as I got.

In the first episode of season five, James and I trolled Katie, Stassi, Kristen, Jax, and Scheana while they were attempting to have drinks to celebrate Katie and Tom's engagement. Randall may be my soul mate, but James Kennedy was my absolute life partner in shitty behavior, and we loved nothing more than getting hammered and behaving like garbage people to those who pissed us off.

We walked up to the group, got into their bottles, started drinking their booze, thinking we were being funny. Then I looked at Katie straight in the eyeballs and said, "I can see that everybody here has *not* been working on their summer bodies."

Katie was stunned. I had a twisted little smile on my face, because I knew *I got her.* She had fucked this season up for me, now she was going to pay.

James, of course, was the perfect foil and took things even further, relentlessly fat-shaming the bride-to-be. "Wait, are you pregnant? Oh my God, congratulations!"

Scheana stood up and told us to get the fuck out of there, knocking James's glass out of his hand. The glass shattered on the ground, and James and I marched away, proud of ourselves, unrepentant. When James and I were drinking, nothing could touch us. Nothing. We were invincible.

To this day, when people ask me what my biggest regret on *Vanderpump Rules* is—and I've had a lot of bad moments—it would be body-shaming Katie. Number one, I think the female body is beautiful—*all* of them. But on the real, I love a full figured woman. Send me Ashley Graham naked on a silver platter, and I would be the happiest girl ever to just stare and admire. But I knew that weight was the one thing that Katie was super insecure about, so that was the thing I knew I could destroy her with. I knew how to attack someone's weak spots, so I called her a no-sex-having Teletubby, and then I told her I was going to fuck her man. I look back and I struggle to recognize myself as that person. But she was me. She was Lala. A heat-seeking missile, set to kill.

Midway through the season, Ariana invited me to fly up to Sonoma in Northern California wine country for her birthday party. Ariana was one of my few allies at the time and seemed to understand that I had this hair-trigger defense mechanism that I couldn't always control. I committed to going, but the morning I was supposed to go, I started freaking out about having to possibly be confronted about all of the lies I'd told and mistakes I'd made.

They were going to shove me in an RV with these people so that everyone could hammer me about Randall, bust my balls for fat-shaming Katie, and tell me that I'd broken up a family, over and over again. No way was I going to put myself through this. I had been drinking too much, my anxiety was through the roof, and I couldn't bear it anymore, so I bailed on the whole thing. Not just the birthday—I bailed on *Vanderpump Rules*, Randall—the whole shebang. Being Lala had become too much for me to handle. It was the Fourth of July, Independence Day, and I wanted my life back.

First, I called Randall and let it rip. "You fucking did this to me! Because of you, I'm being called a 'home-wrecking whore' while you get to hide! I have to go out and fucking deal with this, not you! I want nothing to do with you!"

I turned off my phone, packed up my car, and drove ten hours to Utah, to my parents, where I was safe, where I could be away from everything and my crazy life in LA.

I didn't like who I was becoming. Lala was wearing Lauren down, and Lauren needed a break. Randall was devastated, but I refused to talk to him. I just shut down. I didn't care about the private jets, the fancy dinners, the trips. Being the girlfriend of a powerful man who was in the middle of a divorce *and* being on a reality TV show was too much for me to handle.

I was home for a month, although it felt like a lifetime. I started talking things through with Randall. And I stopped drinking, because I was safe and had no reason to medicate. But I was still adamant about quitting the show, afraid of what would happen to my mental state if I went back into the lion's den. Clearly, I was too fragile for the reality TV life, for LA. Why would I put myself back in that environment, day after day, to the point that I was turning into a drunk? This wasn't me. Even though I knew I was responsible for my actions, there was just something about that group of people that seemed to bring out the absolute worst in me. I hated the feeling of being hated. And I hated that the only way I could handle it was to get white-girl wasted every day. I had to do better.

One day, my mom got the inevitable phone call from the *Vanderpump* showrunner, gently explaining that I had a contractual obligation to the show, and they really hoped I would come back and at least formally quit my job at SUR on camera or they would be forced to serve me legal papers. Basically I had to come back and quit on-screen, or face legal consequences.

"It looks like she disappeared into thin air," he explained. Although I understood, the mere thought of stepping foot in SUR again gave me epic anxiety.

I sat down with my mom and dad. I still wasn't sure what I wanted to do, or if I could face these people, none of whom were my friends. None.

Then my dad said something that proved to me that even though he did not watch the show, he knew what his kid was up to. "I think you should do that thing that you do, what do you call it?" he said. "Give them Lala. I think you should go back and just give them Lala." I knew he was right.

I went back to LA and got ready to say goodbye to the show. I made sure I showed up looking like a snack. To this day, it's still one of my most favorite on-screen looks—legs for days, classy but still a little bit "Who's your mama?"

I told Lisa I was done, and she accepted my resignation from SUR.

"All I wanted was the best for you," she said. "And if this isn't the right place for you, I understand that. You've got to grow from this, Lala."

Then I walked away. I was done with *Vanderpump Rules*. I'd gotten what I needed out of it, and I was good. My name was known; I'd gotten a lead role in a movie; I'd met my boo. Thanks for the good times; see ya around.

I had no interest in appearing on the season five reunion, even though the producers really thought I should do it. Eventually, I realized they were right. I wanted to have the opportunity to say my piece and have the last word. Lala was indeed going to make an appearance. Lala was going to get some closure.

Halfway through the reunion, I walked in, wearing an elegant white pant suit and my grandmother's pearl choker, surprising the rest of the cast. I was nervous, and rightly so, because as soon as I sat down, Katie, Stassi, and Kristen started coming for me. Scheana apologized for the names I'd been called all season. But the other girls seemed unmoved. To them, I was Satan, and to me, they were the holy trinity of basic.

At one point, Andy asked me if I was dating someone, and I answered yes.

He asked if it was the same person I was dating last summer that the cast members had all heard about.

I stayed cool. "Um, I'm not answering that question."

There was some back-and-forth with Lisa, then Lisa talked with Stassi, and Tom brought up how she had done something similar on season three. I said that there was more to it, and nobody needed to know who I was dating because it's not their business, and that's when Stassi said, "Because he's married?"

I felt my rage boil over. "Stassi, enough!" I got out of my seat and told her, "Do not fuck with my relationship, bitch! Fall the fuck back!" Everyone went quiet, and I sat back down. Calm again.

Katie confronted me. She told me how upset she was at the way I'd fat-shamed her and called her a Teletubby. The hairs prickled on the back of my neck, my heart pounded and my heart completely turned to steel as I got ready for whatever was coming my way. Calmly, I told her how upsetting it was to me, being called a whore, and something amazing happened. Katie apologized. Sincerely. And that moment changed the whole game.

Here's something about me: I may be vicious, but look me in the eye and say you're sorry, and I'm putty in your hands. Anyone wishing to deescalate a situation with Lala should know that "I'm sorry" is my absolute Achilles' heel and will instantly turn me into a small puppy who loves you forever.

Tears filled my eyes. I had waited a really long time for one of those girls, any of them, to express an iota of concern for my feelings. I knew I was partially to blame, because I always acted like I *had* no feelings to speak of . . . when the opposite is true. I immediately apologized to Katie for what I'd said to her and explained myself. How there's something about me, how when my feelings are hurt, I'm a pitbull.

Andy, who was probably feeling like a marriage counselor at this point, looked relieved and said he felt like we had made a little headway.

He had no idea how right he was. One by one, as the reunion continued, we managed to work through our problems. It was like group therapy, I swear. The girls acknowledged how their words and judgment had affected me, and one by one, they all began to apologize for their shitty behavior, as I, in return, apologized for mine. So many feels. By the end of it, I can truly say that not only was the air cleared, I walked out of there feeling like I actually cared about these people. Weird.

I began to look at this entire cast of women—especially the self-proclaimed "Witches of WeHo," Katie, Kristen, and Stassi—

less as enemies and more as human beings who, like me, had been thrown into the reality TV pressure cooker, which seems to amplify every single flaw you have.

Stassi told me afterward, "It's so crazy—now I know you; you're still the same person you were before—but my attitude to you is completely different. When you say appalling shit, I just laugh because I know, oh my God, this is just Lala. And Lala just says outrageous shit." I have to say, in that moment, I felt truly and 100 percent understood.

After the reunion, I was in such a good place with everyone that when the producers asked me to come back for season six, my answer was absolutely *yes*. But this time, no more skeletons in the closet. I would respect Randall's privacy, but I wouldn't lie about our relationship. There's a reason they call it reality television, and I wasn't going to put myself through another season of lying and trying to play the system. It just doesn't work that way.

When the time came to shoot, I felt I could finally recognize myself. I wasn't drinking as much, because I felt more relaxed. The *Vanderpump* cast thought I was funny, like my best friends in Utah always had. When you've known me a while, you'll know that when I say crazy, outlandish things, it's not supposed to be taken so seriously. It's just me being silly, trying to make the whole room lighten up a little bit.

Meanwhile, Rand's divorce had been finalized, which meant we could finally start having a more open and relaxed relationship.

He met all the cast members, and everyone loved him. On the show, though, I would only refer to him as "my man."

By the time it came to start filming season six, I'd moved out of the Ho Palace and into the Palazzo, a high-end apartment complex in West Hollywood by the Grove, where Randall had hooked me up with a two-bedroom, two-bathroom apartment, which meant that when my family came into town, they had somewhere to sleep instead of on a blow-up mattress on the floor. The Palazzo doesn't allow cameras inside, so you never saw my apartment in season six—which is a big part of the reason Randall picked it. "Fuck no, there's no way they're filming us hanging out," he said. Which I understood.

Then, right before we started shooting, Faith called me and confessed that she'd made a terrible mistake—she had slept with Jax. What a bombshell to drop on me, and what a difficult position I found myself in. Faith was my friend, and everyone makes mistakes, but I was terrified of the ramifications and how it would affect my relationship with the rest of the group. I had finally made good with these girls, and now Faith was telling me that she just slept with the fan favorite's boyfriend? I knew that this was going to blow up in all of our faces.

My heart broke for Brittany, and the whole thing also was triggering some really bad memories for me. What she was going through, dealing with public humiliation as a result of her man's actions, reminded me of what had happened to me in season five, when the world was calling me a "home-wrecking whore." My man got to run and hide while I took the heat, and this double standard of how men and women are treated was driving me nuts. That's why the whole season, I found myself going toes with everybody's boyfriend, telling these entitled guys to stop treating their girl-friends like trash. Enough was enough.

"I'm sick of these fucking men doing whatever the fuck they want and thinking it's okay!" I yelled, as the cameras rolled.

All the girls climbed on my bandwagon, and whatever our dif-ferences may have been in the past, we definitely formed a united front on this issue. I'd made my peace with these girls, which meant I had their backs, forever. I always say this to people: if you don't like me, then you're really messing up, because no one's going to go to bat for you like I am. If someone hurts you, I'll take the bull by the balls and I'll rip their head off for you. If we're good, I will do that for you. If we're not good, then it's *your* head getting torn off.

When a woman goes out and pursues her dreams, sometimes it makes men view them with fear. Like it's too intense for them to be with someone who could have bigger balls than they do. It's a heavy thing, but I've seen it happen a million times. And these guys are missing out. Some of the most successful women on earth—who are running corporations, who would assassinate any man in business—

they find their power to be a turnoff to dudes, because a lot of dudes are soft. It's really sad. God forbid they're with someone who is smart and intelligent but isn't also a Susie homemaker who's going to cook you dinner, raise your children, and make sure your house is clean.

On the flip side, while powerhouse women are intimidating for men, girls who are working at restaurants, scraping by, are often treated just as poorly by guys, who look at them and say, "Oh, they're beneath me. I need someone who has it together."

So let me get this straight—you want us to run a million-dollar business, raise your children, give you sex four days out of the week, cook and clean, look incredible every single day, and not get mad when you cheat on us? Please.

I've had these conversations with Randall, because I was making very modest money on *Vanderpump* when he met me and living in my dumpy little spot in Miracle Mile. But I paid for everything on my own, I saved, I had a great car, and I never struggled for money; I could afford to go out and spend $100 at the bar, and I often did. I wasn't living the best life ever, materially, but I think he could tell right off the bat that I was a hustler.

He doesn't expect me to cook and clean, and I don't feel pressure to have him fed at night. He knows that I enjoy working on my business, because that's what I thrive from, and that's when I'm happiest. If I told him tomorrow, "I want to give all that up and just stay at home," he would do whatever he could to make sure that I could be a stay-at-home mom. It's easy with us, because what I want is exactly what he will support. It sounds so simple, and yet, it's rare to find.

Season six marked the downfall of my friendship with James. It had been a long time coming. He'd gotten a girlfriend, Raquel Leviss, and in a season-defining moment, James and I got into a giant argument ostensibly because I ate some of Raquel's pasta. The phrase "It's not about the pasta!" would soon enter the fan vocabulary, but there's so much more to the pasta incident, and I'm going to reveal it now, because trust me, it really wasn't about the pasta.

Cast your minds back. We're sitting at the table, having brunch. What the viewers didn't see was the producers, looking at me expectantly, wondering if I would bring up that season's mega gossip with James—namely, that he and his best friend, Logan Noh, had hooked up, as the rumors suggested. I didn't care whether he had or hadn't, so, instead of saying, "James, did you and Logan hook up?" I said, "We ate all (Raquel's) pasta and she didn't give us permission." Don't ask me why. It just seemed like a lighter thing to talk about over brunch.

Well, in hindsight, maybe I would have been better off asking him about Logan, because he totally lost it. In James's day-drunk mind, me casually eating his girlfriend's pasta was a form of bullying, and he clapped back with the most unnecessary, evil venom, calling Randall awful names and bringing up that old favorite . . . Lala's a gold-digging whore. I was so mad, I had to walk out of the restaurant before I flipped the entire table.

James's mouth was maybe more vicious than mine. He'd pull these insults out of the darkest, meanest corners of his subconscious, slap you with them, then laugh. I knew it was mainly when he was drunk that he behaved this way. But in calling Randall those names, he crossed the line.

And that is how this guy, my homie, whose back I'd had through thick and thin, found himself yelling at me in the street: "IT AIN'T ABOUT THE PASTA! IT'S NOT ABOUT THE PASTA!" as a way of explaining why he'd just insulted me to my very core.

James and I eventually made peace, and he shared the stage with me when I debuted my song to close out the season, rapping in his English accent. When we were good, we were great, two peas in a pod. I just hoped and prayed to God the pasta incident wouldn't get aired, because if Randall saw it, it was over for my friendship with James. Of course, the argument aired, and to this day "It's not about the pasta!" is one of those *Vanderpump* catchphrases that just won't go away. Randall saw it and was not amused. At the reunion, I stayed calm and told him, "When you drink you say a lot of things. I can forgive you if you attack me, but when you attack someone I love, it's going to be much more difficult."

No, of course it wasn't about the pasta. It never was. We both knew that. It was about James sabotaging our friendship, because that's what we alcoholics do. James and I became best friends at the best times of our lives, getting wasted every day, starring on TV.

We missed being wild kids together. That's what it was really about. But now, it was time to grow up.

chapter ten

THE DAY AFTER 4/20

I OFTEN LOOK AT PICTURES taken when my dad came out to LA for his birthday in March 2018. It was such a special time for us. I'd hired a sommelier to come to my apartment, who'd brought fine wines and imported cheeses for my mom and dad to sample—my dad loved a nice glass of wine more than anything, and I could tell he was really enjoying himself because he had that old sparkle in his eye. Like I said before, I treasured those moments because they had become few and far between.

On his actual birthday, Randall and I took him for a sushi dinner, and then on to Hyde nightclub, part of which we'd rented out. Randall and my dad's birthdays were only two days apart, so it was a joint celebration, and Rand got Warren G to come to the club to perform. Dad seemed happy, in good spirits, and entertained by his Hollywood birthday, very touched that Rand had gone to such great lengths to create a fun evening, as he always does. My dad had always been supportive of the boyfriends I brought home, but with Randall, he seemed extra relaxed. He knew I'd finally found someone ready and capable to be a partner and who could take care of his daughter. You know, dad stuff.

Which brings me to this: when people say I have daddy issues, I 100 percent agree. I have issues with anyone's dad who isn't like mine. I have issues with any man who can't treat a woman just like my dad treated my mom. I have issues with a man who can't treat his kids the way my dad treated us. My dad showed me what a woman deserves in life. Unconditional love and a sense of purpose and possibility—whether I'd wanted to be the president or a regular joe, I knew he'd always have my back.

When Randall was first getting to know me, it took him a moment to wrap his head around my adoring relationship with my dad. He thought it was a little unusual that I needed to talk to my dad so much, usually every day. Only when I opened up to Rand about my childhood, and all the issues with my dad's health, did it start to make sense. To me, my dad was a unicorn, a walking miracle, a cat with nine lives and a titanium heart valve, and every day he was on this earth, some part of me was thinking, *Today is a great day.*

Two weeks before his birthday blowout in LA, my dad was in our condo in St. George by himself, working. He was managing a job site out there, still trying really hard to find some business that fulfilled him, the way real estate had in the nineties.

In the evening, he went to dinner with our neighbors, who are in their eighties and more fun than most people my age. The restaurant they went to was on a hill, and after dinner, while driving down the hill to get home, my dad suffered a stroke. He passed out and crashed the car into a tree, his foot still on the gas as the car caught fire with him inside, unconscious. People in the restaurant saw what happened, called 911, and someone dragged him out of the car, saving his life.

As soon as my mom found out, she tried calling me, but I was in bed asleep and had left my phone in the kitchen. This is why I now keep my phone under my pillow at night. I happened to wake up to get a drink of water and saw I had a lot of missed calls, most recently from Randall. I called him back and he said, "Lala, I'm on my way to your apartment. Your dad's been in a car accident. He's okay, but he's in the hospital. Let's get you to him."

Stunned and frantic, I stuffed a few belongings into a bag and waited for Rand to pick me up. He drove me to the airport, put me on a private jet to Vegas, because there was no way to land directly in St. George at that time of night. In Vegas, I was met by a British woman from the company that had organized the plane, and a car and driver for me.

She handed me some flowers and said, "I'm so sorry. Get in the car. Go be with your dad."

It was a two-hour drive from Vegas to St. George. The whole way, I watched episodes of *Seinfeld*. *Friends* and *Seinfeld* are my Xanax, because they're just these perfectly engineered moods that cancel out stress and take you into a funny, mundane place that feels very safe to me.

Once I got to the hospital, I was relieved to see that my dad looked normal. His face wasn't droopy on one side, which is common when someone has had a stroke, and there were no physical signs of injury or trauma, even though he'd crashed his car into a tree on the edge of a cliff. What a miracle, this guy! But even though he seemed fine, I couldn't help but worry. My dad was just shy of sixty-four years old, which is still young in my opinion, but he was no spring chicken. And I remembered hearing how oftentimes, after people have strokes, things can go downhill quite fast. I wasn't ready for that. Losing my dad was my nightmare, my deepest, darkest fear, and had been since I was a little girl. My dad was this smiling, happy force in my life, but there it was again, the fear, lurking, the unspoken understanding that no matter how much my dad said he felt okay, he could be taken from me at any second. And I had no power to stop it.

My dad stayed the night at the hospital, and when we went back in the morning, he was doing great, really chirpy, cracking jokes. They had moved him out of intensive care and into a regular room, and one of the nurses on the ward was a big fan of mine. She asked me for pictures, which I was fine with. But then she kept coming in the room, snapping pictures of me sitting by my dad's hospital bed. My mom talked to one of the senior nursing staff and asked them to stop. Most of the time, I love interacting with anyone who connects to me in a positive way. But there really is a time and a place to ask for a selfie, and in the hospital, while my dad is sick, is definitely not it.

Two days later, he was out of the hospital and back at the condo. The doctors didn't want him traveling for a week and a half, so instead of going back to Salt Lake he stayed put. He just hung outside, watering the lawn, reading and relaxing while getting his strength back. I figured we would cancel his LA birthday, but he insisted on coming and wanted to carry on as usual. As always, I was relieved, and amazed by how resilient my dad was.

———

On April 20, 2018, a month after his party, I was having a fun day. It was 4/20, and I was posting videos of Destiny's Child, looking super stoned in an interview, young Beyoncé saying if she could be any animal she'd be a whale. Funny shit. I had been talking to my dad every day, as usual, and when I'd called him that day he seemed to be doing okay—Randall had a BMW i8 that he'd sent back to Utah for Easton to drive for a while, and my dad said Easton was out front, washing it, all excited to drive it. I asked Dad how he was feeling, and as usual, he said he felt fine.

Later that day, my mom called me. "I'm really worried about Dad," she said.

"Why, what's up?" I asked.

"He's very lethargic and hasn't been eating, but I can't get him into his cardiologist for a month." A month was way too long to wait, considering he'd just had a stroke, so after our phone conversation, Randall made an appointment for my dad to see his cardiologist in LA the following Monday. That Monday would never come for my dad because by the next morning, the morning of April 21, 2018, he was gone.

I woke up and saw I had a few missed phone calls from Easton, which was unusual because he is definitely not a morning person. I called him back, and he said the words I'd hoped I wouldn't have to hear for a very long time.

"Hi, Lala. I hate to tell you this, but Dad passed away this morning." His voice quivered as he spoke.

"No, no, no." I just kept repeating the word, over and over. This wasn't real. I couldn't be twenty-seven and not have my dad anymore. This wasn't happening to me.

I made my way from my bedroom to the kitchen, where I broke down. I called Randall, and as soon as he picked up, he said, "I'm on my way to you right now, baby." He had already been told the news. I called Madison, who'd always had a special relationship with my dad. Come to think of it, everyone did. My dad made everyone feel like he cared about them, and it was never an act—he genuinely did.

"Madi, my dad just died," I said, my voice trembling.

She was speechless at first. Then, quietly: "I'm on my way."

Randall and Madison arrived, and we were out the door. Randall had chartered a jet for us so we could get to Salt Lake as quickly as possible. On the way to the plane, I asked Randall to stop off at the liquor store for a bottle of vodka. When he got back in the car with the liquor, I opened it and started drinking out of the bottle, desperate to numb myself. I did this from morning until night, for the six months that followed.

The flight to Salt Lake was a blur; I have no real memory of anything until we were pulling into the cul-de-sac, to the house I grew up in, where a crowd of people was standing outside. I got out of the car, my mom walked up to me and collapsed in my arms. I remember her looking into the sky, hysterical, asking my dad, *"Why? How could you leave me?"* She blamed herself for his death and said she wished she had taken him to the emergency room the night before he passed. "I was supposed to protect him," she sobbed, and I comforted her.

Her pain was immeasurable. As human beings, I believe God has built us to be able to cope with the death of a parent; it's the circle of life. But to bury our children, or handle the death of our life partner, is different. My mom lost the love of her life, the father of her children, the man she had been with for thirty-nine years. There was nothing anyone could say to ease her suffering.

We didn't want to be in the house, so we went to the Grand America Hotel, in downtown Salt Lake. My older brother, Brandon, met us there with some of our childhood family friends, and all we did was cry and share sweet memories of my dad. I felt schizophrenic, smiling and laughing at some warm memory only to break down again, numbing myself with cocktail after cocktail. In the end, my mom and I decided to stay at the hotel; we just couldn't face being at the house without Dad being there. Easton wanted to go home, so he left my mom and me and we checked ourselves into a room. I took three Tylenol PMs to knock myself out and gave my mom the same. The next morning, we both opened our eyes, looked at each other, and immediately started sobbing. Somehow, it felt even worse than it had the day before. This wasn't a nightmare; this was real life. My dad was really gone. He was now someone who only existed in my memory.

Today was going to be a throwaway day, we decided. My mom and I were going to stay in a dark room, drink all day, cry, and watch TV—except Randall wasn't having it. He came into our room, pulled open the drapes, and spoke words I will always remember.

"Wake up, ladies. I knew Kent, and he wouldn't allow this. We're going to go to breakfast, and pay tribute to him. He deserves that from us." We knew he was right, so we got up, I chugged a small bottle of Grey Goose from the mini fridge, and we went to Gracie's, one of the last places in Utah I'd gone to with my dad.

Two days later, I posted about my dad's passing on Instagram, sharing a video I had taken of my dad, my mom, Easton, and me in the car, when he'd come to LA for his birthday. I'd used one of those funny filters that gives you mouse ears and a squeaky voice. It was so surreal watching it, knowing he was gone. We had been having the best day ever, and only our higher power from above knew that in a month, it would never be this way again. The caption read:

"Rest in paradise, my sweet dad. The world seems to be spinning much slower. I've never felt so lost. I've never felt so sad. My world has crumbled."

I often go back through my Instagram feed and look at this moment in my life. How my page goes from being lighthearted, the post from 4/20, where I'm giving my stoners a shout-out, to something very different. Who would have known the next day my life would never be the same?

Two weeks after he died, all the girls from the cast flew into Utah to come to my dad's celebration of life, which meant so much to me. The gathering was held at the Porcupine Pub, a homey spot my dad would go to every Monday and Wednesday night to meet his guy friends for drinks. They gave us the top of the restaurant for free and provided all the food, and I was completely overwhelmed by the number of people who showed up to pay their respects.

Randall had reached out to all of my mom and dad's close friends and made a video set to the sound of "Forever Young" by Rod Stewart. My dad loved to play that song when we went on road trips in the car. Even now, when I listen to it, it brings back a lot of good memories, but that day, when the video came on the screen, I couldn't handle the emotions. I told Randall I had to leave, and the wake continued without me.

Afterward, Randall took my family and our close friends to Las Vegas. He was acting as our bereavement concierge, doing his very best to take care of us, keep us connected to one another, and ensure our minds were occupied. That's what we wanted and needed. I remember walking through the casino at the Wynn hotel, and "Forever Young" came on, and it triggered me so hard I broke down in the middle of the lobby. I collapsed sobbing, and Randall had to pick me up and take me back to the hotel room. I've always been an emotional person, but this was different. It ached in my bones. It took the air out of me. It made me sick to my stomach. Denial, anger, bargaining, depression, acceptance—all the five stages of grief spun around my head at once. He can't be gone. . . . Why is he gone? . . . We can't go on without him . . . but now we have to. Somehow.

The night after the wake, Randall got us Utah Jazz tickets, because we wanted to do anything we possibly could to take our minds off the fact that he was gone. At the game, I got super fucked-up. I can't remember what I yelled at one of the players, but everyone turned around and looked at me. Someone said, "There are children here. What are you doing?" My mom, I remember, was mortified, but she had my back—she told the woman sitting behind us that I had just lost my dad, and everyone understood.

I had to get away from them all, so I got up and walked up the stairs to where the concessions were. I started crying and screaming, "I have to get the fuck out of here. I have to get the fuck out of here!" So we left the game and took bicycle taxis back to the hotel, me and mom in one, Rand in the other with Easton. I was still drunk out of my mind. We told the bike taxi guys to race. I remember my mom and I were belly-laughing, like lunatics. Once we got back up to the hotel room, I grabbed a pillow and put it over my face and started screaming at the top of my lungs. I was so angry. I didn't want to be in Utah any longer. We had said goodbye to my father. Now it was time to leave.

My mom and I flew to LA, and after we got back to my apartment at the Palazzo, everything was a fog. My dad was gone, but I couldn't grasp the thought that he only existed in my mind now. That I would never see his face again. That I would never feel him hug me, and that his hugs are only a memory. I kept listening to his voice mails, over and over again, anything to fool myself into believing that a part of him was still here.

Every few hours I would pop to Ralphs supermarket to get a bottle of champagne for me and mom. After a while, we realized one bottle wasn't going to be enough. So we'd walk from the Palazzo to Ralphs and each get a bottle. Then two bottles each. Both of us were just fucked-up, all the time, anesthetizing ourselves from the horrific shock of having lost the beating heart of our family so suddenly.

Later, the coroner would tell us that they didn't think it was a heart attack—my dad's body had no signs of tension, typical of someone who has had a massive heart attack. He said it appeared my dad left this earth very peacefully. I tried to find comfort in that, but it did little to erase the feeling that a huge hole had just been blown into our lives. The foundation was gone. We were like a chair with three legs, useless, off-balance without him.

We decided against performing an autopsy—my dad had been cut open and prodded from the time I was eight years old, and he needed to be left alone now, finally. Nonetheless, I requested his medical records from the hospital in St. George, where he'd been admitted after his stroke. I wanted to see if there might be a link between the treatment he received there and his subsequent passing. In his files, I noticed it said he had diabetes, which was news to me. I was sad that he'd been dealing with that, on top of everything else. It's possible he didn't know, but knowing my dad, it's possible he did know and had been hiding it, because he didn't want to worry us. The thought crushed me. But it was too late now. He was gone. . . .

I started filming season seven of *Vanderpump* three weeks after the death of my dad. I'd had nothing like enough time to even begin to process. I probably should have taken time off, but oddly, *Vanderpump* felt like a source of stability, and I felt like my dad would have wanted me to carry on. I showed up with a new look, dark brown hair, a reflection of how I was feeling inside; darker, like a different person. Because I was so emotionally fragile, I decided to give up drinking during the time we filmed. No one on the cast understood how heartbroken I was, or what I was going through, and that was partially my fault. I wish I could have been more vulnerable. I wish I could have asked everyone to handle me with kid gloves, because that was what I needed. But I didn't.

Some nights I would dream about my dad, but they were never happy dreams. They were always stressful and heartbreaking. In one, we were on a train that was out of control, my dad lying on a gurney and people saying they couldn't save him and were about to push him off the train as I screamed, "We have to save him!" In another dream, he and I were in a car, my dad seeming to lose control of steering, and I was frightened we would crash. My subconscious was forcing me to relive my pain, my panic, my sense of helplessness.

I've always asked myself questions about God. Do I believe in a higher power? When we die, do we just become dust? After my dad passed away, I began searching for answers to those questions with greater urgency. Sometimes, I wondered how it could be that I was still alive, still breathing through this pain. That's when I decided that when people die, they don't just go into the ground; they become a force that you can't even explain. A force that helps the people they love. I have the strength that I have today because my dad is up there, doing a lot of work on my behalf. Don't ask me how I know, I just do.

One day, I walked into SUR feeling on the verge of burning the town down. Billie Lee was holding her weekend brunch, and I remember wearing my hair in a high half pony and a not-so Dolce and Gabbana–looking jungle print dress that plunged down to my belly button. I've never admitted one giant secret about that day, until now—before I got miked that day, I was next door at Tortilla Republic, a Mexican restaurant, sneaking drinks. I had committed to staying dry during filming, but that morning I woke up just knowing it was going to be a rough day, and my solution for that was alcohol. So I hung out at Tortilla Republic, drinking champagne. I thought drinking would help, but all it did was add fuel to the fire that raged inside me.

During brunch, I heard Raquel, James's girlfriend, refer to my dad's passing as an excuse, and I lost my mind.

"Do not ever fucking bring up my dad!" I yelled at her, my finger centimeters away from poking her eye out. "I thought you were a fucking dummy before my dad died, you fucking Bambi-eyed bitch!" Afterward, I sat and cried angrily to Brittany, and when Billie Lee approached, I exploded with more venom and words I didn't mean.

Billie asked me to leave her brunch, and I continued on my rampage, saying, "Not only are you boring to speak to, you're boring to look at, too."

Her comeback was "Your dress is 1995," and to call me a psycho.

The look I had on was actually 2000-era JLo at the Grammys, but I definitely was psychotic in that moment, I'll agree with her on that. She kept following me, until eventually I turned around and told her to "get the fuck out of my face, ho!" while trying not to headbutt her. I hate calling someone a ho in an argument, and why I chose that word to throw at her on more than one occasion during filming is still unknown to me.

The grieving process is a tricky thing. It's not something people can talk you through, or calm you down from. It happens the way it happens, and it will be different for everyone. My projectile venom toward Billie and Raquel wasn't about them—anyone could have said the same things they had, and my reaction would have been the same. Do I regret how my words affected them? In that moment, no. Although right now, in my sobriety, I am learning how to take accountability for my words and actions. At that time, though, I was in a fog, in survival mode. I wasn't able to think about how I was affecting people; my goal every day was just to get out of bed and put two feet on the ground. I was brimming with raw emotion, and I felt so alone, as do many people who have gone through bereavement, because our society just doesn't know how to talk about death. People like to pretend it's not there because it makes them uncomfortable. My rage toward what I saw as other peoples' insensitivity was probably better than the alternative—depression—and the desire to just drive my ass over a cliff. Would I have ever gone through with something like that? Probably not, but to say I never thought about it would be a lie.

Only a handful of people tried to understand why I was losing my mind—like Katie, Stassi, Brittany, and Kristen. No, they didn't condone the way I was lashing out, but they tried to empathize with why it was happening. When I opened up, they let me talk. They were there for me as friends, watching as, somehow, I showed up at SUR every day, a smile forced across my face, even though bubbling beneath the surface was a volcano, ready to blow.

chapter eleven

BREAKING THROUGH
HURRICANE-PROOF GLASS

FILMING *VANDERPUMP* IS ALWAYS a tumultuous experience, full of ups, downs, and surprises. My rational mind knew that I couldn't get super drunk, or drink at all, in fact, after my father died because I needed to be in charge of my emotions. I had not recognized my alcoholism at that point, but I understood that alcohol would probably make my grief harder to deal with, and that's why I decided I had to try to stop for a while. It didn't last.

When my mom and I drank champagne at home in the immediate aftermath of my dad's death, we were in shock, and my mom was mourning. As soon as she went home to Utah, she went back to her normal life, stopped drinking, and began to deal with her grief. I, on the other hand, did not. I'd wake up to go to the gym and have a glass of champagne before I left the house. I'd stop at Ralphs on the way to filming to buy coffee cups and a bottle of Veuve, and drink the whole thing in the underground parking lot. I would be late to work, but I thought that was okay, because at least I was taking the edge off my emotions. At work, I would put champagne in a coffee cup and sneak a drink, or go next door and slam margaritas by myself. All this, while pretending to everyone I was sober.

By the time I got home every night, I'd be so fucked-up I sometimes worried I might drown in the bathtub, or fall and hit my head in the shower, because I never went to bed without brushing my teeth and bathing. No matter how fucked-up I was, I always managed to wash my body and my face and brush my teeth, and I usually chose the bath. Once I was in bed, I would proceed to smoke weed and drink until I fell asleep, making sure to keep the champagne bottle next to my bed so that when I woke up, I could start over. Instead of morning coffee, morning champagne, please. Rinse and repeat.

I kept telling myself I had to stop, but then I'd go out and get drunk again. Eventually, I'd tell myself that it was okay, that maybe I just liked to drink, and when I had babies, it would all calm down, I would change and be a "normal" person again. I was in complete and utter denial that I had a problem, a problem that was spiraling out of my control.

Randall was the only one who knew how much I was drinking,

so we made a pact to be sober together for a while. I'd go out at night and sip water, keeping it straight, sticking to my side of the bargain, thankful to have Randall as a sobriety buddy. One night, I met up with him after an evening with friends and could immediately tell he had been drinking. I was furious, betrayed—we'd made an agreement, and I needed my partner to take it seriously! I was so pissed, I told him I was taking a break from the relationship. I walked out of the house, and he followed me, begging me to stay. As I was getting into my car, in what remains a weirdly cute memory for me, Randall snatched my Gucci slides right off my feet and threw them on the ground, as if I couldn't drive without shoes. He should have taken my keys.

"Keep the fucking slides, I'll see you later," I said, slamming my car door and driving away.

I didn't care about anything anymore, except that my dad was gone. I cared that I could no longer call him up and ask him what the right thing to do was, because I was really beginning to lose my grasp.

Toward the end of the season, I started drinking in front of my fellow cast members again while on a trip to Mexico, during which I got fucked-up to the point where my anxiety was so high that people were worried about me. I made Scheana and Kristen hold my hand and stroke my cheeks at an outdoor restaurant because I was sure I was having a panic attack. I wanted them to tickle my arm, or scratch my arm, do anything to make me feel something other than wanting to crawl out of my own skin.

When we got back from Mexico, we filmed the finale and I announced, once again, that Lala was going to stop drinking. In a conversation that never aired, I told Stassi that I believed I had a problem and I was going to start going to AA. That didn't happen, though, because I wasn't ready. I was still too blind to myself, too confused, to do the right thing. The only thing that felt safe was Randall, and before long, we were in each other's arms again.

At the beginning of mine and Randall's relationship, it was all fun and games; we were busy having the best time ever together, because we truly enjoyed each other's company, no matter where we were. But shit got real when my dad died and my drinking escalated. Added to his divorce, and the pressure of me being on a reality TV show, the roller coaster we had so enjoyed at the beginning started to feel like a terrifying ride neither of us could escape. At times, it felt like we were addicted to the chaos as much as we were to each other. Above all, I refused to question my relationship with alcohol. As far as I was concerned, if anyone had an issue with my drinking, that was their problem, not mine. I could regulate it, I thought. I used alcohol as a crutch during filming, or when things got hard in my life. If I needed to take a break, I could. It was that easy, or so I thought.

Randall had planned on proposing in April 2018, the month my dad died, and had gotten my father's permission before his death, but obviously he had put the proposal plans on hold until I was able to find some sort of stable footing again, emotionally. In September, after shooting wrapped, he took me to Cabo for a birthday vacation at the Esperanza resort. We were in a good place, especially because I was on one of my infamously short-lived breaks from alcohol. I hadn't had a drink in a month, since the Mexico trip with the cast.

On September 1, the day before my birthday, he said he was going to take me out for a pre-birthday celebration. It didn't cross my mind for one second that he was going to propose, especially because I had always told Randall that anybody who proposes on someone's birthday is cheap—you want your birthday to be special, and you want your engagement to be special. Separate days, separate things.

We walked down the beach where a cabana had been set up, just for us. This was classic Randall, always pulling off some magic to make me feel special. The sun was setting, and happy as I was, I grew very emotional about my dad—this was my first birthday without him, and I couldn't shake the feelings of sadness that he was no longer around. Randall pointed to the sky and I looked up—there were clouds, floating above our heads, in the shape of a hand holding a heart in the air. Randall said it was a sign that my dad was with us, and immediately, I felt a little better, because I knew he was right.

After the sun set, Randall said he wanted to take a walk along
the beach, which seemed like a strange idea because it was so
dark, but I went with it because I just wanted to be wherever
Randall wanted to be. He was my birthday gift; he was my everything.

We walked down the beach and he led me to a spot where
some couches had been set up in front of a big screen and pro-
jector. I couldn't believe he'd arranged a second beachfront setup
for us.

"This is your birthday surprise, Lala," he said. "We're going to
watch an episode of *Friends* on the beach and roast s'mores." This
was perhaps the cutest thing anyone had ever done for me in my
life. I'm obsessed with *Friends*, that's my happy place, and Randall
knew that.

Friends came on the screen, and we got all cuddly on the
couch. Then the screen blacked out, and Randall said to the assistant, feigning annoyance, "Are you kidding me? This is her birthday present! Get *Friends* back on the goddamn screen!"

The assistant kind of smiled, and then something popped up
on the screen—not Ross and Rachel, but a montage of my life with
Randall. Photos and videos of me with his kids, me with my dad,
us together, the whole progression of our relationship, and at the
end, the words, *This is only the beginning*. It wasn't until he pulled
the ring out that I realized this was more than just the most incredible birthday surprise I'd ever had. There he was, on the sand on

one knee, reading me a letter that he'd written, describing the conversation he'd had with my dad right before he passed away, making a beautiful speech that ended with the words:

Will you be my wife?

A photographer came out, ready to capture the moment where I accepted. But I was speechless. No words came out of my mouth. I was a willing prisoner of this moment, the most beautiful moment of my entire life, and I had no intention of leaving.

"Lala, I'm going to need you to say yes within the next thirty seconds," Randall said.

I snapped out of it. "Oh! Yes. YES!"

Right as I told Rand I would be his wife, fireworks went off along the entire beach, and the effect was like something out of a movie. For the first time since my dad died, I felt like that night, I was able to celebrate something good.

In the morning, as a chef made us breakfast while we laid by the pool, Randall, no longer my boyfriend and now my fiancé, came up with another brilliant idea. "Lala, all of your friends are in Las Vegas. Should we go there, instead of staying here another night?"

So we fueled the G5 and we were out of Cabo, off to Vegas to meet up with my castmates. We celebrated my engagement, and my birthday, with the people I loved the most, not including my family and Randall's daughters.

Although they didn't know that we had gotten engaged in

Mexico, Rand had been sure to run the idea by them first, and luckily for me, the girls were very much in favor of the idea. Rand showed me the video of how excited they were when he asked how they felt about him proposing. In fact, they said *they* wanted to ask me to marry their dad, so when we got back from vacation, I gave Randall the ring back. He wrapped it in Saran Wrap, and he and his girls hid it in a cake, just for me. When they presented me with the cake, I acted surprised to find the ring.

"What is this?" I asked, unwrapping the ring.

"You're gonna be our dad's wife!"

Even now, the girls tell people that they asked Lala to marry their dad.

I was wrapped up in Randall's perfect proposal and the promise of a happy future, and it felt like our roller coaster was on the up and up again. But relationships can't survive like that, on a permanent high. Not forever.

When season seven started airing in November, it triggered a lot of feelings for me, feelings that caused me to crash right back to where I was before. Seeing those episodes forced me to relive my dad's passing all over again, and I was being inundated with hate from viewers, who mocked my wild mood swings and called me out for my venomous insults, which, to be fair, were totally out of control.

Every Monday when the show came on, I would drink, heavily, then I'd look at comments online, searching for ones that weren't terrible. People who had experienced their parents' passing seemed to understand what I was going through, and their words kept me going. They understood that bereavement is messy, and it goes beyond just being hurt. They knew that it can shatter the very foundation you walk upon, your sense of self, your idea of what the future looks like. They related to how it ends your innocence and forces you into an adult understanding of our mortality that can be unbearable. But not everyone has gone through that kind of loss. And it's impossible to expect them to understand how grief can turn you into the darkest, least reasonable version of yourself.

"Your dad dying is no excuse for your behavior," someone wrote.

"Your dad would be so disappointed in you," said another.

These were the words that I shouldn't have allowed myself to read. But I did. I saw them. And because I wasn't capable of rational thoughts at the time, I took it all on board. Before long, I hated myself more than I'd ever hated anyone. And as usual, I turned to my faithful friend alcohol to help me handle the shame.

I would look at myself in the mirror, drinking from a bottle of vodka, and ask myself, *Would my dad be proud of me acting this way?* I had no idea. All I knew was that my dad, someone who I thought would be there when I got engaged, when I got married, when I had babies, the person I had always pictured being part of all of that, was gone. I felt guilty, and questioned myself for being happy about getting engaged, when just a few months ago, we'd cremated my father. I was juggling too many emotions—guilt, shame, longing, sadness—so I stayed drunk all the time to avoid feeling them. The drunker I got, the more I took everything out on Rand. This man, who had loved me so unconditionally and supported me through the worst time of my life, became the target of all my rage because I had nowhere else to put it.

At least once a week, mad drama would go down between us. I'm talking relationship-ending, call-the-cops kind of drama. I think the first real escalation came when we got in a loud screaming match one night, over something so dumb I can't remember what it was, and he locked the bedroom door on me. I kicked through it, unlocked it, grabbed his phone and threw it on the ground so hard it shattered. Then I went to his kitchen and took all of his premade meals out of the fridge and drop-kicked them all over the floor and walls. The next day we made up, and Randall forgave me for getting so heated. It happens. It's love. That's what we told ourselves.

Not long afterward, we were in Atlanta, where Rand was shooting a movie. We went to a strip club and were having the best night ever until I had one too many and crossed the line from "I feel amazing" to "I'm going to assassinate everybody." Randall must have said something, I can't remember what it was (that was the running theme of our arguments: me being too drunk to remember how they started), but when we were walking back to the hotel from the strip club I chucked my phone at him, which I then lost.

(Later, the bouncer from the strip club called my mom and said he found it in a parking lot, and sent it back with my ID and all my credit cards.)

Back at our hotel room on the seventeenth floor, our arguing continued to rage. I threw his wallet off the balcony. Then I put his duffel bag in the bathtub, turned on the faucet, and let the water soak all his belongings. I slipped on the tile, cutting and bruising my knees, while pulling out his drenched luggage. I heaved the soaked bag to the balcony and threw that over, too. Nothing was spared. Even his shoes got tossed, seventeen stories down, and I probably would have thrown everything in that room off the balcony, had we not heard a knock on the door and a voice saying, "Open up. Police."

I looked at Randall and whispered at him to shut the fuck up. I quickly put on lingerie and a sexy little bathrobe, messed up my hair, and made myself look cute, as far as I could in my inebriated state. I answered the door.

"We're getting a lot of noise complaints," said the cop.

These weren't hotel security—these were full-on cops with guns and badges. I stayed perfectly calm.

"Oh my gosh. I'm so embarrassed, we like to role-play," I said. "I'll make sure we keep it down."

Miraculously, they bought it, and left. I closed the door, looked at Randall, and started laughing. Nothing felt real anymore. It was all a game.

The next morning, I felt terrible about what had happened, so I went downstairs on my own to look for his belongings that I'd hurled out the window the night before. I searched and searched, but everything had been taken. *Everything.* We were supposed to be leaving that day, and now, thanks to me, Randall didn't even have a pair of shoes to walk out of the hotel in. I went to the hotel spa and asked them if they sold men's flip-flops.

"We have slippers," the woman said.

"For men?"

"No, only women's."

I bought the spa slides, very feminine, and Randall wore lady slippers to the airport and we caught the jet back to LA. On the plane we held hands and kissed, it was as though nothing had happened. Randall is much more patient than me. He receives my moods gracefully and always tries to make things better. When he gives me attitude, I'm less forgiving. I'm not patient, and I can be a bitch. Anyone who didn't end up with me should pat themselves on the back, because they dodged a huge bullet. Randall truly is the gem of the relationship, and especially during the dark period of time after my dad died. I was two different people. Sweet, sober Lala—the woman Randall had fallen in love with. And the other Lala. The beast.

Every time I drank and something happened, I'd wake up in the morning feeling horribly guilty, then we'd work through it, and by the afternoon, we'd be laughing about it. Randall always had a way of babying me out of my guilt. But the depression, nothing seemed to cure. Depression, when you're in it, feels inescapable. You can't shake off the moody blues, unless you're too drunk to realize you're having them, which is exactly why alcohol continued to make so much sense to me, at the time.

Privately, Randall was starting to have serious doubts about our future. But I was too fucked-up to notice or even know what was happening in real life. I was floating in an alcoholic fog, entirely detached from any sense of what I was feeling, and from what other people were feeling. My empathy was at zero, and I was completely out of tune with every emotion, except the one telling me to order another drink, buy another bottle, down another shot. That's alcoholism. That's what it does to a person. It takes away the bad feelings, but it also erases the most beautiful parts of being human.

There are many different expressions of alcoholism; I learned that when I got into AA. Not all alcoholics hide bottles in their closet. Not all alcoholics drink every day. But one thing all alcoholics do is affect other people in a negative way. People who coexist with alcoholics and find it in their heart to forgive what they've done . . . those are some really special angels, I'm telling you.

Meanwhile, the fights with Randall, my angel, continued to escalate. When I was drinking, you could look at me the wrong way, and all hell would break loose. Randall could be sitting there quietly, and I would suddenly decide I didn't like the way he was breathing. That's all it took. One night in Miami I took all his clothes, shoes, and toiletries and threw them into the pool before taking his toothbrush and putting it in my asshole for a minute. Later, when Randall came out of the bathroom, brushing his teeth, he asked me why I was laughing.

"That toothbrush was just in my asshole," I said, and the look on his face, a combination of sadness, hurt, and disgust, will forever haunt me. I'm sad to say that was not my lowest point. The worst was yet to come.

This is all so mortifying for me to share, but I have to, just to remind myself why I gave up drinking, and why a nice girl from a nice family would do something like putting her boyfriend's toothbrush in her ass. Alcohol, plain and simple.

When I first got sober, I would think about the things that I did, especially to Randall, and I couldn't bear it. I was so embarrassed, so ashamed. I'm glad that he and I have gotten to a point in our relationship where we can laugh about some of these moments. We laugh hard at the fact that all of this happened but also that we were crazy enough to keep going. To say, "Yeah. Let's stay together. This is totally healthy."

Another night in Miami, we were at a club called LIV at the Fontainebleau hotel, and I was, as usual, super fucked-up. We were sitting at the DJ booth while he talked to some guy and I talked to his girlfriend, who was bisexual and feeling up my leg.

Have I hooked up with chicks before? Yes. Ask Ariana, whose

cookie I nibbled in the back of her car while her boyfriend was driving. But do I actually go both ways? No, I don't. So for me, her rubbing my leg was no big deal.

Randall saw things differently and told me we were leaving the club, which irritated me. A sober Lala would have sat her man down and made him feel comfortable and had a normal conversation. But drunk Lala didn't want to stop partying just because some girl rubbed my leg and Randall thought it was inappropriate. When someone tries to stifle my fun is when I go cray-cray. Ruin my good time, and that's when I see red. We argued the whole car ride home.

When we got to the house, I stripped down naked but kept my heels on, and continued to fight. Poor Randall went outside to get away from me, and I chased him, naked except for my heels, running circles around the house, screaming at him for ruining my fun time. He ran inside and locked the door; I tried to get in, banging on this thick glass door, and when he didn't, I smashed the heel of my black Christian Louboutin against the glass over and over until it shattered. I don't know how, because that was some thick glass. But I managed to break it, and then the argument ended as quickly as it had begun—drunk Lala usually gets to a point where she's tuckered herself out, like a baby who's thrown a temper tantrum, then all of sudden, it's nap time. So after smashing the glass with my heel, I went inside, went upstairs, got in the bath, got into bed, and fell fast asleep.

The next morning I woke up and kissed Randall. "Hi, good morning, baby."

He looked at me. "Do you remember what happened last night?"

"No. What happened last night?"

He took me downstairs and showed me the shattered glass on the floor. "Do you remember doing this?"

I covered my mouth with my hand, mortified, as the memories flooded back. "Oh my God. Yes."

When the glass-repair woman came over later that day, she looked at the broken door, surprised. "How did this happen? This is hurricane-proof glass. It's supposed to be indestructible."

It may have been hurricane-proof, but I guess it wasn't Lala-proof.

Again, you might think this is where I bottomed out and finally realized I had to get sober. Nope.

Not long after, Randall and I took steps to try to understand why our relationship had become so volatile. We met with a psychiatrist, and my drinking came up during our first session. The psychiatrist asked Randall if he would please leave the room so she could talk to me privately. When he did, she gave me a phone number.

"This person is a case manager for alcoholics and drug addicts," she said.

"Are you asking me to be sober?" I said. "Because if you are, that is out of the question." I told her I had come to terms with the fact that I just like to drink. I'm fun. I enjoy having a good time. And that's that.

She said, "I'm not asking you to do anything. I'm asking you to just put this number in your phone, in case you ever need it. You may never need it. But if you do, you'll have it."

Fine, I thought. *Whatever.*

A few days later, Randall and I left for Disney World, with a group of twenty-six people. Randall's kids, sister and niece, his parents, my brothers, my mom, my niece and nephew—a whole crew—and of course, I was shit-faced the whole time. We were staying at the Animal Kingdom Lodge, a short drive from Disney World, and every morning, before we left to go to the theme park, I would go down to the bar, get my vodka pineapple, chug two there at the bar, and take one for the road. Always a roadie. While everyone was enjoying the rides, I would be constantly bugging everyone to go to the bar. My family, sure, they were down to have some cocktails, because they were on a vacation. For them, it was just fun. But for me, it was different. I was trying to numb myself . . . in the happiest place on earth.

One night, we were at Planet Hollywood for dinner and I stumbled down the stairs, in front of Randall's dad, who has been sober for more than twenty-five years. My mom helped me back up the stairs, and when we sat down, I looked at her and said, "Mom, I need to go to the bathroom but I'm really, really drunk, so I need you to walk me there." So she walked me to the bathroom, and then walked me back down the stairs when we finished. I had drunk myself into such oblivion, I could no longer function.

The next day, back at Disney World, it was business as usual, and I drank all day again. And again, the next day, I was ripped. That evening, we were heading back to LA and I walked into the gift shop, my eyes glazed over. Every alcoholic knows the feeling, when you've been on a bender, drinking nonstop every day, and you're in that awful place where even though the sun's out and you're with family and there are little kids everywhere, innocent and smiling, you're somewhere else, moving in slow motion through life, with no idea what the hell is happening. Today, there are times where I'll see people who are drunk, and something in their eyes shifts, even though nothing has changed in the environment—it's the alcohol, shifting their perception. They're hearing things differently. They're taking peoples' words the wrong way. People are laughing and having a good time, but suddenly they think people are laughing at *them*.

At the gift shop, Easton bought a bottle of Hennessy, and I fixated on it. I wanted that bottle to drink on the plane. Before we left, I went down to the bar, did my two face chugs of my vodka pineapple, and then I took a roadie in the car to the airport. Once we boarded the plane, I repeatedly asked Easton for the bottle of Hennessy, which he eventually pulled out of his backpack and gave to me. I began chugging straight out of the bottle on the plane and spent the flight hysterically crying one minute and laughing the next, playing voice memos of me singing on my phone, from years ago, forcing people to listen, telling them to shut up when they weren't paying enough attention.

At some point, the kids got restless, so I let them draw all over my legs with pen and marker and put lip gloss all over my face. By the time we got back to LA, I looked like a sad, drunk clown. Randall could not handle me anymore. He dropped me off at my apartment, went home with his kids, and that night, he wrote me a letter calling off our engagement. He planned to give it to me at the office the following day. I had pushed Randall's love to its very limit—and for someone who has oceans of love in his heart to give, that's saying something. But I was spiraling, hard, and Randall couldn't bear to watch anymore. I don't blame him.

I got ready for bed. I sat in the bath, scrubbing my legs until my skin was red and raw, removing all trace of the pen and marker, desperately trying to erase all memory of what had happened on that plane ride and how drunk I had been in front of Randall and both our families. The next morning, I woke up, alone, and opened my eyes, staring up at the ceiling as a montage of my life flashed through my mind's eye. All the drunk, angry moments, the fear, the ever-increasing rage I felt in my heart replayed in my head, showing me the story of someone who has been in denial for a very long time. Someone who needs to change. I felt my father's presence and heard him say to me, "This is not you, Lala. This is not okay. You have to do better."

I sat up, and the truth hit me, clear as crystal.

Bitch, you're an alcoholic, I said to myself, and immediately, a weight lifted from my chest. It was October 22, and I'd had my last drink on October 21, exactly six months after my dad died.

That morning, I went to Randall's office. I said I wanted to talk to him in the conference room. He came in, sat down, and waited to hear what I had to say. I took a deep breath, and tried to steady my voice.

"Randall, I'm an alcoholic, and I can't live like this anymore. I'm so sorry for everything I've done. I am going to reach out and get help today."

Randall's eyes filled with tears, and he nodded and told me he loved me. He didn't give me the letter he'd written the night before. In fact, he didn't tell me about it until months later. On my one-year sobriety birthday, Randall offered to show me the letter, and I told him I wasn't ready for it yet. I asked him to hold on to it. I did want to read it at some point, but there is a time for everything, and I felt that this wasn't that time. Knowing how close we came to losing each other still sends shudders down my spine.

After leaving the office, I called the number that the psychiatrist had given me.

A woman answered, and she said she was a case manager. I told her I needed help. "I want to meet with you on Thursday, and until then, I want you to call me every single day," she said.

That Thursday, I went to her office and I told her my story.

"I want you to think about going to rehab," she said. "I think that it could be very beneficial to you."

She showed me a bunch of different places to look into, but I wasn't sure. I wanted to think about it. I decided to put rehab on hold while I tried working the steps at AA meetings.

"But if I do pick up a drink again, I'll have no choice but to go and check myself in somewhere," I said.

"Sure," she said. "Put it on the back burner. If you have a relapse, then we'll revisit rehab."

She hooked me up with an AA sponsor who got me going to meetings. I read the Big Book cover to cover, and started working the Twelve Steps. Quitting alcohol was the hardest thing I'd ever done, and my first meeting, I felt utterly defeated, like a lost soul. I couldn't understand how all the people there looked happy and acted so friendly toward me and one another. Then I listened to their stories, and I realized they all had to get to the sad, lost place I was at now before they were able to get happy again.

As the days passed, I began to regain clarity. I started asking myself the question: *Why? Why do I drink? Was I born with the gene that predisposes you?* When I lived in Utah, I never acted like an alcoholic; I probably went out and drank twice a month, tops. I was a normal drinker. My mom's great-uncle had passed away from alcoholism, I knew that much, but we didn't seem to have much alcoholism in the family. We had no idea if addiction existed on my dad's side of the family, since their Mormonism meant alcohol was never in the picture.

I traced the years of my life and tried to understand how my relationship with alcohol had shifted over the years. When I moved to LA, I was living my best life but I wasn't an angry drunk; the turning point seemed to coincide with the beginning of my time on *Vanderpump*. To be clear: I am in no way blaming the show for my alcoholism. *Vanderpump Rules* remains the greatest, most life-changing opportunity I have ever been given. But what reality TV does is expose you to the realities of yourself. And my reality was that I was doing vodka sodas at 10:00 a.m. before filming because I didn't know how else to manage my anxiety. Then, right after I met Randall, and during season five, when I was being called a home-wrecking whore, my disease seemed to have really kicked into gear. And by the time my dad died, there was no stopping me from finishing a bottle of vodka during the day if I wanted to. Alcoholism crept up on me, stealthily. It's not a disease that takes hold overnight. It takes its time, twisting you around its little finger, until you are powerless against it.

Back when I was drinking, I remember feeling like Randall was very controlling. He always wanted to know where I was at all times, and if I was with certain people, he got very upset. Now, I'm sober and I can understand why he was acting protective. He was traumatized that every time I went out, I'd get fucked-up, something weird would happen, then I'd come home to him. It was a shit show. Now, I go out and text him at two in the morning and it's no big deal. He trusts me.

Therapists have asked me to dig into my past, and the bullying, and I still have trouble connecting it with my present-day reality or my alcoholism. I'm okay with it. It happened, but I'm not affected by it on a day-to-day basis. I got bullied like many children do, and everybody deals with it differently. And once I was out of high school, I didn't feel damaged, I felt great. For me, what happened is that I started drinking every day, and all of a sudden it was something my body needed; my alcoholism is a progressive disease, a physical and emotional addiction that developed over time.

Some well-meaning people tell me that maybe when I'm older, I'll be able to have a glass of wine. I wish that were true. I just don't have that luxury anymore. I abused that privilege, and it has been taken away. Every alcoholic has a little devil inside them, telling them they're more powerful than alcohol. But I have a disease, and this disease knows no cure. It will awaken any time I decide to pick up a drink, and in order to keep it under control, I'll have to steer clear of it for the rest of my life. It's a daily battle, but every time I struggle, I remember how close I came to losing the love of my life. No drink is worth that.

When I stood up at an AA meeting and said I was thirty days sober, everyone clapped and went insane. It may sound like a short period of time, but those first thirty days represent a huge milestone for any alcoholic. One woman at the meeting, who I love and adore, came up to me and said, "Lala, you look so different. There's a glow about you. You look like you're in a good place. I hope I see you here every week."

A year and a half later, I still go to that meeting, every Sunday.

chapter twelve

GIVE THEM LALA

*E*VER SINCE I WAS young, I always wondered why Beyoncé would go by Sasha Fierce when she got onstage. Why did she sometimes need an alter ego in order to perform? Then I listened to an interview of hers, where she talked about how Beyoncé is this timid girl from Texas and Sasha Fierce is this bad bitch who sells out arenas.

"I have someone else that takes over when it's time for me to work . . . and that kind of protects me and who I really am," she said.

I am by no means Beyoncé, but I can relate to the idea of creating a separate identity to protect yourself, out of necessity. Bey has to step into a different zone so people can listen to her music and love her, but she can't allow them to get too close to who she really is. If she does, what's left for her? Similarly, I, Lauren Burningham, had to transform into Lala Kent in order to allow complete strangers to see every detail of my everyday life, because if I had put Lauren from Utah behind the hostess station at SUR, she would have been eaten alive. Lauren could never have lasted on a reality TV show, but when she stepped into Lala's shoes, she became confident, a bad bitch otherwise known as Lala, patron saint of public meltdowns. God bless her soul.

Only people who are very close to me know Lauren, and they know just how soft she really is. My family and my best friends whom I've known since we were babies—they've seen me with my walls down, after Lala kicks off her glass-shattering Louboutins and relaxes back into someone a little less . . . extra.

But Lala is a whole other creature. The minute I get a text telling me where I need to be for filming, Lala comes to life, like a robot being powered up. Lala understands she has a job to do, and Lala doesn't need a script, because Lala is not a character—she is the Amazon warrior version of myself.

When she joined the show in season four, people took her at complete face value. They were offended and turned off, which was confusing to me because I'd never gotten that reaction back in Utah among the people who knew and loved me. My friends back home thought I was hilarious and understood that most of what comes out of my mouth is just a joke, an attempt to get a rise, because I've always been a bit of a clown, a provocateur, who really just wants to make you laugh. Being misunderstood forced Lala to evolve into a tough bitch who made her thoughts and feelings clear. I was an outsider, and once I realized the girls on *Pump Rules* were coming for me, I wasn't going to baby their feelings, and I sure as hell wasn't going to show them my tender side.

I used to say if you don't love me at my Lauren, you don't deserve me at my Lala. But these days, it's not so simple. I used to think that Lala was the shit. That she was more fabulous than Lauren. But now, after everything I've been through, I've come full circle. I've had to get back to my roots, and in doing so, I've realized that's what I'm most proud of. I am proud of the chick who got herself sober. Who got through her dad dying. And that wasn't Lala. That was me. Lauren from Utah.

There were days when I would watch myself on TV and think, *She's so badass*. It was like I was watching a different person. And this *may* be the most narcissistic thing that ever comes out of my mouth, but sometimes I inspire myself when watching myself. I think, *Oh my God, who is that? I wish I could be that ballsy!* Then I realize, I am. I look at Lala, with all her faults and all her mistakes worn proudly on her sleeve, and I'm proud of what she's become. Because she's living her life in a way that Lauren would never have had the courage to.

Lauren needed Lala, but Lala needs Lauren, too. There's a happy medium there, somewhere, where I can be a strong and independent person but not become hardened by the things that life has thrown at me. Every heartbreak, every sad moment. All the things that are embedded in my DNA, including the pain of what we went through with my dad's health and, later, his passing. Lala never opened up about those things because she doesn't trust the world and thinks you have to be a tough bitch to survive. But it's exhausting being on the defensive all the time. Recently, I've been wishing that the side of me you see on TV could be softer, less intimidating, less abrupt. Maybe a little more like the core of who I am. A little more like Lauren.

Not long ago, I was talking to a famous and accomplished actress, Kathrine Narducci, who starred on *The Sopranos*. She knew me as a reality star and was surprised when I told her I had booked a role in a thriller starring alongside Bruce Willis. I confided in her that I was excited but extra nervous; I was mainly used to being Lala in front of the camera, and Lala sucks at being vulnerable on-screen, which is exactly what this role required. She gave me some important advice that day.

"Whenever you go and do a scene, I want you to search for Lauren," she said. "I want you to picture her, find her, and let her guide the way."

Soon, I was on set, shooting, digging deep for emotion. I searched for ways to express and emanate those feelings that I usually keep buried deep inside. When the director said "Action," I pictured little Lauren, and my dad holding her hand, and immediately, I was where I needed to be. From then on, before every scene, I kissed my hand and rubbed my heart-shaped *DAD* tattoo three times and thanked my father, Kent Burningham, for always guiding me, whether he's in the room or not.

———————————

The editors on *Vanderpump Rules* are phenomenal at what they do and at helping us share our story. They're the reason we have a show that keeps people coming back for more, season after season. But sometimes, the show doesn't tell the full story of who I really am. That's okay, it comes with the territory of reality television. It is what it is: entertainment. I don't get any input, nor am I able to see the episodes until they air, so in that sense, I'm just like any other fan when a new season drops, sitting on their couch at home, wondering what fresh hell Lala's going to find herself in this week. It's like an out-of-body experience, watching yourself, realizing what's coming out your mouth.

Because I never know what version of Lala is going to be broadcast week to week—am I going toes, or just having a seafood dinner with Rand—it means the fans' opinion of me can literally flip-flop from one week to the next. I've seen it happen in DMs—after an episode where Lala is presented as a heroine braving tough times, fans will write me heartfelt messages and show me so much love. Then a bad episode airs, and those same fans will say, "You're not the person I thought you were, please kill yourself."

Fan love is easy come, easy go, and can be taken from you after one bowl of pasta, one basic brunch with Billie. The people who love you may love you because of one episode they saw. The people who hate you may hate you because of one episode they saw. Haters become stans, and stans decide they despise you. I have no control over whether a fan is willing to empathize with what I'm going through and love me unconditionally, so that's why I have to approach fan love the way I approached men during my ho phase—don't get *too* invested, and don't take anything personal, or you're always going to be disappointed. Just do you, have fun, and let Lala handle things, because Lauren is in no way psychologically equipped for this emotional shit show.

For a long time, I wanted certain parts of myself kept off-limits. There were things I thought belonged inside my sacred zone. Then I realized those were the exact things the viewers found most interesting, because they're going through the same things in their own personal lives. All the skeletons in my closet had to come out in order for me to properly do my job. Reality TV offered me a platform; I had to step up and talk about my struggles in life. Reality TV showed me what being a role model actually means and how, oftentimes, it's not about being perfect. It's about being *imperfect* and then being willing to talk about it.

Sharing things about my alcoholism, for instance—that was not an easy thing to do on TV. But people love those skeletons, so these days, it's like Halloween out here—skulls, bones, heads on pitchforks out front, every inch of my life, proudly on display because there's nothing left to hide. I'm willing to put myself out there and be naked because there's healing that comes from living your life in the open. Darkness loses its power when you expose it to the light.

Had it not been for reality TV, I would never have had a reason to go that deep with myself and face up to my truths. That I have a tendency to turn to alcohol when things get bad. That when I feel insecure, I turn into a raging bitch. That even when I'm not drunk, it's easy to push my buttons. If I hadn't gone through *Vanderpump* bootcamp and seen myself laid bare, I might never have had the opportunity to rise above it and work toward becoming a better person.

I'm not the only person in the world struggling with addiction. I'm not the only person in the world mourning the loss of her dad. I'm not the only person in the world who takes things out on her partner when she's drunk. But I'm one of the few people in the world who can share it all on TV. Even if I'm judged for that, it's worth it to me because there might be one person out there who sees me, recognizes themselves in me, and finds something to hold on to, to laugh at, to give them hope, and show them that they're not alone. I'm walking proof that people can have the handbags, the private jets, and the Gucci slides, and still be sad because that doesn't cancel out the addiction, the anxiety, and the depression every day. When people feel me on that level, it helps me feel less alone. It makes me realize that we're all connected.

It's very intimate, this relationship I have with strangers. Some of the things people share with me are intense and put me in a position of responsibility that I take very seriously. I get DMs from people in dark places with their addictions, at make-or-break moments in their lives. It's an honor that they feel able to turn to me. I get DMs from people letting me know that my little skeletons have helped them out, and those messages are what keep me sane and positive throughout my day. So every day I try really hard to focus on the love, and if I get a little bit of hate, I'll toss it after ten minutes, just like my mother taught me.

Now, let's discuss trolls. I've learned, like the rest of my cast, that trolls will eat you alive if you let them; they're like walkers from *The Walking Dead*; they don't stop, and when they're mean, they're meaner than I could ever be. And yet, I don't mind them. They're very loyal in their hate. They're the ones who keep coming back for more. I always say, "Haters are just confused appreciators, sheep in wolves' clothing."

The best haters are the ones who can't get enough of you because they're so hooked on hating you. They're watching every episode and talking about it online. They're tuning in and listening to your podcast, because they're dying to rip you a new one every week. Without our devoted haters, we wouldn't have a television show, I wouldn't get to sell makeup or have a podcast. So I give my haters—all of them—a lot of love.

That being so, Randall and I did have to invest in permanent security, and when we get super-creepy messages, we send them over to our guy, who does a background check immediately, to see if these people have a criminal record that we need to be aware of. Private security doing background checks on scary DMs, just to keep us safe—yes, that's what it's come to, and that's really the only downside of all this. I think it would be different if we didn't have kids, but when you've got precious babies running around, that really changes the game.

Here's a fun fact: when I get a really shitty message, like extra mean, I check to see if they're following me before I decide whether to block. If they are following me, I won't block them, because I'm not willing to lose a follower over some petty BS that happened in this week's episode. I allow them to keep hating, knowing they might change their mind the next day. But if they *don't* follow me and they're sending hate, then I block the hell out of them, because, like, why are you even here, breathing my air? The real assholes, the ones who say things that cut really deep, usually aren't following me. I'm talking about the ones who say they love watching me cry about my dad because that's my karma and they're happy that he died. I don't let that kind of talk slide. It's so offensive, so wrong. And I usually let them know. I'll write them something along the lines of "Wow. God is looking down on you, thinking 'damn, I really fucked up with one.'" And then they get a block.

One girl went insane on me recently, calling me a dry drunk, saying that just because I'm sober doesn't mean I act like it. Listen, becoming sober doesn't turn you into Jesus; I know I'm not walking on water or turning the other cheek—just because you stop drinking doesn't mean you stop being a human being who reacts to things. The only difference is, you're in your clear head, which can be either amazing or very scary, especially if you're still acting out when you're sober and working a program—something that came to my attention about myself in season eight. It's a hard awakening to have, because when you're working a program you have nothing to blame your actions on anymore, except yourself.

I sent this girl a message back, saying, "Please fuck off, babe," and she responded with a very different tone of voice, saying she had just listened to my podcast and now she understands that I need love right now, that I'm still grieving and need to be handled with care. Which just melted my heart. I then responded with a friendly message, because it felt like we'd gone through something, then worked things out, and gotten to a place of understanding.

Another girl sent me a mean, toxic message, and I DM'd her back, saying, "Hey, cut me some slack."

She responded, "Oh my gosh I didn't realize you were a real person."

It's fun, being able to respond to people and help them realize that "wow, this is a real human being." Because sometimes people really think you're just this made-up character they watch on TV, with no real feelings. But believe me, all the feelings are real.

If Reality TV is God, then the networks are the different saints and angels. Maybe you worship E!, or maybe you're part of the Bravo cult. That's why there is a BravoCon, because the people who are watching *Vanderpump Rules* aren't just watching that show; they're tuning in every single week for a new episode of Housewives, *Below Deck*, and *Southern Charm*. They have every night of the week scheduled for one of their Bravo shows, and they know their favorite Bravolebs inside out. For these people, BravoCon is their wet dream, a three-day Bravopalooza where Bravo influencers can meet the superfans. *Ten thousand* of them, under one roof, wanting to experience their favorite shows in real life. It's more fun than Mormon church, I'll tell you that.

The *Vanderpump* cast flew to New York, where there were already fans hanging out in front of the hotel. Just by looking at them, I could tell that BravoCon was going to be lit. There were so many of them, you would've thought we were Destiny's Child in their heyday, or the Beatles.

I called Randall, excited, and he teased me, saying, "You love that shit."

Of course I love that shit. Throw me in a situation where I'm treated like I'm Lady Gaga, and I'm not going to complain. I'm going to be very happy to be immersed in that level of fan love.

The next day, we went to the venue, and even though I was totally sober, I got a contact high being around these people, all of them having so much fun. I was connecting with people from all walks of life, because even though I come off as an entitled bitch sometimes—my whole *I'm a queen, you're a peasant, fuck off* attitude—that's just part of Lala's act. It brought tears to my eyes that there were people in that room who had saved up for months to go to BravoCon, to hang with one another, and have a chat with us. It was humbling.

James was DJing the *Vanderpump* after-party, and five hundred people showed up, packing the room. They put the cast members up on a balcony, and I remember looking out, seeing everyone holding their phones up and recording what we were doing. All I could think was, *I love these people so much!* Without them, I might not have found the love of my life. Without them, my childhood dreams might not have come true the way they have. I was completely overwhelmed with emotion, and I was so glad to be sober, so I could feel it all, and know I'd never forget.

The next day, we did a panel with our daddy, Andy Cohen, and I kept hearing people from various parts of the theater screaming "Give them Lala!" It was surreal, hearing my little catchphrase being chanted by strangers in a room. This was, hand on heart, bigger and more profoundly fulfilling to me than I could have dreamed. More affirming than any acting role. Actors don't display their real selves to the world—they do a junket, talk about a role, and keep their guard up. Unless they're very unique people, like Mickey Rourke or Lindsay Lohan, they're not going to show themselves to you drunk, screaming in the street, face chugging margaritas, sucking on a bubba, and still expect to be loved for it. Which made me think, maybe this *was* what I was supposed to do all along. I wasn't Mary-Kate or Ashley, I wasn't Beyoncé, or any of my heroes. My fans loved me and were here because I gave them Lala. Pure and simple. No script necessary.

On that stage, for a moment, I lost all sense of space and time. Andy Cohen asked me a question, and I didn't hear a damn word he said because I was so in love with what was happening in front of me. To be in a room full of strangers who know everything about you, and love you for it, at least some of the time. And then, I saw him. The *WWHL* kid, in the crowd, wearing a Give Them Lala sweatshirt that he had made himself. The kid who had always shown me so much love and always shown up to take a picture with me outside the *WWHL* studio, each and every time I'd appeared. In the five years I'd been on *Vanderpump*, he'd always said the same thing to me the six or seven times we'd met. How much I'd helped him with his anxiety and with embracing who he is, because he'd really struggled with confidence and being able to love himself. I didn't even know his name, but by this point, he felt like family.

I waved, and beckoned to him to come up onstage. That kid, like the DMs I get from people going through addiction, reminded me that this may just be entertainment for some, but it's so much more than that for me. It's what life's about.

Everything I'd ever gone through had led me to that moment, I think: of looking out at this crowd, feeling the love, and seeing the kid with the camera, the kid who had grown up with me and never lost his faith because he was probably going through the same challenges I was, suffering with his anxiety and self-image, and not liking himself very much; being around people who can't understand you and who make you wonder if you'll ever feel safe enough to be yourself.

But in that room, I think he and I felt like we could be ourselves and be loved for it. Finally. In that room, I think maybe we all felt that way.

conclusion

*W*RITING THIS BOOK, I obsessed over every detail, worrying about how the readers might react to some of the stories, wondering, *Will people understand? Will they be sympathetic? Will they love or hate me for what I have shared?*

In the end, though, I can't control how people feel about me. I can't control whether they want to see me happy, or whether they want to see me crash and burn. The truth is, I *did* crash and burn, because that's exactly what I needed to do. If I hadn't hit my bottom when I did, I might not be experiencing the happiness I am right now, aged thirty, preparing for the most important role I will ever play—motherhood.

I think about the baby growing inside me, and I wonder how

my daughter will feel when she's old enough to pick up this book and take a look inside. Hopefully she'll laugh. And hopefully she'll understand a little more about her mother and why she is the way she is. Because writing this book has helped me understand myself in ways I never did before. This book has given *me* Lala and released me from so much of the guilt and shame I used to carry around.

For years, I lived life on the defensive, my fists up, fighting to correct the lies and misconceptions about me. Well, now I can finally say I'm done with that. This book will be entertainment for many, but for me, it's my release. I will no longer explain why I am the way I am, and I will no longer defend my relationship. The truth is all here, and the shame is gone. I have earned my place at the table, and I've accepted that I belong. How I got here doesn't matter anymore—what matters is that I'm here. And I'm happy.

acknowledgments

To MY MAMA, MY brothers, and my sweet late dad; the people who taught me true love and what it means to feel safe and good enough. I love you.

To my fiancé, Rand. We made it, baby. You would have to live in my heart to know how much I love and adore you. And to my daughter, you've taught me so much, and you're not even here yet.

To my Utah girls, Madison, Dani, Olivia, and Candice—I have always felt safe enough around you to be the truest version of myself, and that has been such a gift. You've known me since I was a little girl, and you have no idea what you've given to me on this journey. Thank you.

ACKNOWLEDGMENTS

To my editorial team; Natasha Simons at Simon & Schuster, Tess Callero at Europa Content, and my word copilot, Caroline Ryder—thank you all for helping me share my story.

To Karen Kinney, you are my soul mate and my angel. Thank you.

To Lisa Vanderpump, you changed my life, and I will be forever grateful.

To the cast and crew of *Vanderpump Rules*—what a ride. I wouldn't change a single thing. Not even the pasta.

And to the fans of our show—without you, none of this is possible. Thank you, sincerely, from the bottom of my heart.

CPSIA information can be obtained
at www.ICGtesting.com
Printed in the USA
JSHW030851140623
43148JS00001B/1